S0-AFT-245

CHOCOLATE 💍 CAKE

Marriage

The Recipe to Refresh, Revive and Restore

MICHELLE SULLIVAN

Praise for *Chocolate Cake Marriage*

"Michelle Sullivan has a powerful way of communicating important and life changing issues couples face, today. Her words empower, equip and encourage couples to follow God's recipe for creating the sweetest of marriages. Using Biblical principles, Michelle pours out wisdom, page after page. Every couple will benefit from reading *Chocolate Cake Marriage*. The tools Michelle offers will help readers find deeper intimacy and establish richer communicable skills, producing vibrant marriage relations both in and outside the bedroom."

LaTan Roland Murphy
Author of: ***Courageous Women of The Bible*** (Leaving Behind Fear and Insecurity For A Life of Confidence and Freedom)

"Everything that I needed! *Chocolate Cake Marriage* helped change my perspective on my marriage. This book is real, raw and it doesn't sugar-coat who we should be as a spouse. This past year has been a rough one and Michelle gave me tools to help shape the future of my marriage. I am so thankful for her desire to share with others what the Lord has shown her through trial and error. Michelle has a gift. The words on these pages came at the perfect time."

Carin Schaller
Women's Ministry Secretary, Calvary Chapel Chino Valley

"Michelle lives every word of her message in her everyday life. Her words ministered to me offering deep understanding of how to respect my husband. Her sweet and genuine approach opened my heart to understand what it means to respect my man practically—even offering practical ways to talk to him. *Chocolate Cake Marriage* gives every woman the opportunity to have this marriage changing wisdom. "

Tracy Russell
Key-Note Speaker, Award Winning Author

"Michelle gives very practical tips to improving any marriage. Starting with taking ownership of your part in the relationship, putting Biblical principles into action and trusting change will come."

Becky Hamilton
Operations Manager, **Soul Surfer and Company, LLC**

Copyright © 2019 by Michelle Sullivan

All rights reserved. No part of this publication may be reproduced, distributed, or transmitted in any form or by any means, including photocopying, recording, or other electronic or mechanical methods, without the prior written permission of the publisher, except in the case of brief quotations embodied in critical reviews and certain other noncommercial uses permitted by copyright law.

Unless otherwise indicated, all Scripture quotations are taken from the Holy Bible, New Living Translation, copyright © 1996, 2004, 2015 by Tyndale House Foundation. Used by permission of Tyndale House Publishers, Inc., Carol Stream, Illinois 60188. All rights reserved.

Scripture quotations taken from the New American Standard Bible® (NASB),
Copyright © 1960, 1962, 1963, 1968, 1971, 1972, 1973,1975, 1977, 1995 by The Lockman Foundation Used by permission. www.Lockman.org.

Scripture and/or notes quoted by permission. Quotations designated (NET©) are from the NET Bible® copyright ©1996-2017 by Biblical Studies Press, L.L.C. All rights reserved.

Scripture taken from The Voice™. Copyright © 2012 by Ecclesia Bible Society. Used by permission. All rights reserved.

Scripture taken from the New Century Version®. Copyright © 2005 by Thomas Nelson. Used by permission. All rights reserved.

Scripture quotations marked (TLB) are taken from The Living Bible copyright © 1971. Used by permission of Tyndale House Publishers, Inc., Carol Stream, Illinois 60188. All rights reserved.

Scripture quotations marked MSG are taken from THE MESSAGE, copyright © 1993, 1994, 1995, 1996, 2000, 2001, 2002 by Eugene H. Peterson. Used by permission of NavPress. All rights reserved. Represented by Tyndale House Publishers, Inc.

Scriptures taken from the Holy Bible, New International Version®, NIV®. Copyright © 1973, 1978, 1984, 2011 by Biblica, Inc.™ Used by permission of Zondervan. All rights reserved worldwide. www.zondervan.com The "NIV" and "New International Version" are trademarks registered in the United States Patent and Trademark Office by Biblica, Inc.™

Scripture quotations labeled AMP are from the Amplified Bible, copyright 2015 by The Lockman Foundation. Used by permission. (www.Lockman.org)

Scripture taken from the New King James Version®. Copyright © 1982 by Thomas Nelson. Used by permission. All rights reserved.

Cover design by Alyssa Jackson
Cover photo by Africa Studio/Shutterstock.com
Interior Design and Photography by Danielle Stickel

CHOCOLATE CAKE

Marriage

The Recipe to Refresh, Revive and Restore

MICHELLE SULLIVAN

... I found the one my heart loves.
Song of Solomon 3:4

Dedicated to my amazing husband, Sean. He is my greatest human source of love and encouragement. Besides Jesus, he is the first to tangibly show me what it feels like to be cherished.

I love you past the stars, my love.

Contents

Acknowledgments

Go through His gates, giving thanks; walk through His courts, giving praise.

Offer Him your gratitude and praise His holy name.

- Psalm 100:4 VOICE

Though my name is noted as author of this book, I share that title with so many who I am deeply grateful to for their invaluable inspiration, untiring encouragement, and tremendous patience in waiting for this manuscript to be complete.

Trying to thank all of my sweet friends who have cheered me on this journey to finish *Chocolate Cake Marriage* is like trying to count grains of sugar on a teaspoon—I could try to do it, but I would miss some and not have the full count. You know who you are, and your hours spent pouring into me, sending encouraging notes and texts, nudging me to complete the task are treasures in heaven. Some of you sat across from me with latte in hand to share your heart and story for this book and have been a blessing beyond measure.

I am deeply indebted to Sandy Brown, Rebecca Emenaker, Lisa LaBine, Jill Fawcett, Lisa Parker, Bethany Jett, Michele Palma Koschel, Ken Gaub and LaTan Murphy for their timely input and edits. And to my sweet sisters Alyssa Jackson and Danielle Stickel for their amazing graphic and design talents. God used you all to turn these pages of water into wine.

To my amazing sons, who had to live through tumultuous times when marriage was not done God's way. I adore you and am so blessed to get to be your Mom. Thank you for the grace, love and adventure you pour into my life. I cherish every minute we spend together.

Love and thanks to my dear parents, Dad and Catherine, who truly have a Chocolate Cake Marriage. Your devotion to each other and love for us makes my heart sing.

For his untold moments of encouragement and prayer, thank you to my precious husband for always knowing when I needed to be whisked away on a date night, or given hours of quiet time to sit and write. You are my forever love and my greatest source of courage.

My heart bursts with gratefulness to my heavenly Father and His precious Son, Jesus Christ. You have truly blessed me beyond what I could ever ask or imagine and words cannot express my appreciation. This book is born out of Your heart to have our marriages be a picture of how Jesus loves His church. Praising You for Your mercies that are new every morning, and Your incredible sacrifice that we can have life in abundance because of what was sacrificed on the cross of Calvary. I pray this book brings You honor and glory.

Then call on Me when you are in trouble,

and I will rescue you,

and you will give Me glory.

- Psalm 50:15

Foreword

Absolutely nothing happens by chance with God. In fact, however you came to read this book was meant by God. He wanted this book to be read by you. I've never said that about another book. I feel that strongly about it.

When I first met Michelle, I knew God had something special in mind. I sensed immediately she loved the Lord and He had some big plans for her life. (Feeling He has big plans for you, too, reading this book). I really believe this could be a best seller as word gets out. Thousands of people who are unhappy and discouraged with life, feeling there is no hope at all, especially with their marriage, can have hope that God is going to turn things around in their marriage.

Michelle's early life was headed down hill, with partying, drugs and then a marriage that was messed up to say the least. As I said, when I first met her, I felt God had big plans for Michelle. God even put an Angel in her life or no doubt this book might never have been written. This unusual book is so down to earth and exciting that you won't lay it down once you start reading it. Michelle tells the truth about her first marriage and her failings in life. It made me smile, laugh and shed a tear.

Chocolate Cake Marriage will grab you. The Bible states in Philippians 4:7 that God will guard your heart and your mind. Yes, this book will bless your heart but will also help your mind and affect your marriage for the better. You will go from bitter to better.

I have written seven books, but I have never been as excited about a book like I am about Chocolate Cake Marriage. I believe this book is going to help a lot of marriages that otherwise might end in a mess.

Chapters like, "The Angel Made Me Do It", "Lord, Fix My Husband", "Honey, I've Got a Headache", "The Secret Ingredients", "Roommate to Soulmate", and of course, "Passion Between the Sheets" and all the other chapters will challenge, bless you, and even spice up your marriage.

Many pastors are out there helping families with their marriage situations. This book will help them in their counseling and teaching. Every pastor should have several copies in their office to give to couples to read, even before they start counseling.

This book is the perfect engagement gift. It could solve problems in advance, as well as help those already on the marriage journey. This book is a must read for all.

Ken Gaub,
President, Ken Gaub Ministries
Author, Motivational Speaker
Presidential Award Recipient from President Ronald Reagan
Medal of Merit from President George Bush
J. Edgar Hoover Gold Medal Award for Distinguished Public Service

*Delight yourself also in the Lord, and He will give you
the desires and secret petitions of your heart.*
Psalm 37:4

Sweet sister, this book is written for you. I know marriage can be difficult, but God wants to use your marriage to glorify Himself. As you delight in Him, He will love you, walk with you, encourage you and do above and beyond what you could ask or imagine. Let's join Him on the journey.

One

The Angel Made Me Do It

Don't forget to show hospitality to strangers, for some who have done this have entertained angels without realizing it!

- Hebrews 13:2

ave you ever entertained an angel? Live and in person? Based on God's word, I knew it was possible, but I didn't think it would actually happen to me. I'll give you the facts, and let you be the judge.

Back in 2011, my fiancé, Sean, and I were planning our wedding day, and we decided upon the beautiful island of Hawaii for our destination wedding. A dear friend of Sean's, Pastor Francis Kamahele, is a pastor on the island of Oahu, and we both felt he was the man we wanted to marry us. On top of that, a dear friend of mine knew the manager at the Westin Moana Surfrider in Waikiki, so we were blessed to book our honeymoon suite in this luxurious hotel for a fraction of the advertised cost. Famous for rooms with lanais overlooking the Pacific Ocean, incredible banyan trees throughout the property, and Egyptian cotton sheets in all the bedrooms, we were fortunate beyond measure to call this place home for seven days. It all felt "meant to be!"

On the morning of the big day, my soon-to-be-husband walked to the Moana from where he was staying so we could spend a couple hours together and savor the excitement of all that was about to happen. In the hotel's coffee shop, we talked about the details of the day and dreamed of what would happen in a few hours—our wedding ceremony and getting to be one. I'm not sure which event we were more excited about. We had remained pure throughout our courtship, and we were definitely burning with passion! We both still had a few last-minute things to do, so we finished our coffee, kissed our goodbyes, and promised to see each other at the altar later that afternoon.

My hair and makeup stylists weren't due to arrive for a couple more hours, so I decided to spend some quiet time with the Lord in my room with its incredible ocean view. But as I walked through the foyer, I heard the Lord speak to my heart, "Go out onto the porch in the front of the hotel."

The porch was in the exact opposite direction of where I was heading, so I stopped in my tracks, looked up and thought, *Hmmmmm. I was going to go up to my room to spend time with You, but instead I will do a 180-degree turn and head in the opposite direction.* Curious about what awaited me, I made my way to the porch, a lovely place for vacationers to lounge in oversized chairs overlooking a scenic courtyard and the Pacific Ocean.

The warm Hawaiian air blew through my hair as I glanced around for an open seat at one of the dozen or so dark wooden tables. All the chairs were occupied, except for one. However, a young African-American gentleman, focused on his book, already sat at that table. As I approached, he looked up and smiled. I quietly inquired if he minded if I took the available seat, and he quickly motioned for me to sit.

As I nestled into the large leather chair, having almost forgotten that the

Lord had guided me there, I noticed the young man's book was a black, leather-bound Bible. Hawaii is not exactly the Bible Belt of the Pacific so this was an unusual scenario. "That is so cool that you are out here reading your Bible," I said. "I've come here to spend some time with the Lord as well." I held up my iPhone which was opened to my Bible app. What happened next is what makes me believe I was conversing with an angel, or at the very least, a messenger from God. "So, what do you like to do?" the young man inquired. "Hike? Or write a book?" Those were my two options. Hike or write a book.

He couldn't have known I had written seven chapters for a book on marriage several years prior. The files were on my home computer, neglected and ignored when life got in the way. Somewhat dumbstruck, I stammered, "Ah, yes. In fact, I have started to write a book." To which he replied, "I know. That is why we met today. You need to finish the book."

> I know. That is why we met today. You need to finish the book.

Did he really just say that? How could he have known the unfinished manuscript weighed on my mind? How could he have known I had a passion to encourage women in their marriages and in their journey with God? Plus, to have these words spoken on *this day*, the day I would be exchanging marriage vows with the love of my life—a man I was certain God brought into my life to restore the years the locusts had eaten.[1] And now a complete stranger tells me, "You need to finish the book."

I poured out my appreciation to him for how much his words blessed me because I had been praying about whether or not the Lord wanted me to finish the book. He then asked if he could pray for me. Without hesitation, I said, "Yes, please! I am getting married in about five hours." He prayed the most beautiful prayer over me as though he knew my heart and the broken road I had traveled to get to that day. Later during our ceremony, our pastor prayed many of the same words which made the prayer even more spectacular and God-sent.

"You need to finish the book."

The young man's simple statement is a large part of why this book is in your hands today. Writing a book can be a daunting and intimidating journey. But with God, all things are possible.[2] When the Lord instructs His kids to finish a task, He will be faithful to complete it. [3] Ask Noah. He didn't hesitate when God told him to build an ark. He didn't delay the start of the project until he had completed his "Boat-Building" degree. He didn't wait until he retired and had time to build. He didn't wait until it was more convenient to begin sawing wood and pounding nails. "Noah did everything just as God commanded him.[4]" I am not as bold and brave as this courageous boat-builder. There were hesitations, delays, and inconveniences that got in the way and delayed completion, but I did press on like my brother, Noah—despite my insecurities.

We don't know for sure if Noah experienced some of those same feelings of uncertainty as he undertook such a tremendous faith test. But I suspect that perhaps in his own human frailty, as he waterproofed the umpteenth piece of gopher wood with gawkers jeering at him, he needed to remind himself once or twice that God had called him to the task.

We do know that Noah walked in close fellowship with God[5] and simply trusted that if he kept to the mission, he would complete what God had asked him to do. That was my prayer as well. Lord, help me to complete the task you have called me to undertake.

In no way am I suggesting that writing this book comes anywhere near the quest to build an ark. However, like Noah, I am doing as the Lord commanded me in writing this book. God intentionally led me onto the hotel porch that morning and chose to use a sweet, young man to spur me on to completion. Each time I experienced doubts (and computer troubles, illnesses, time constraints, editor critiques, and the storms of life) and felt like I couldn't actually finish, I replayed the scenario when God led me to hear those words:

"I know. That is why we've met today. You need to finish the book."

I pray God will use these pages to encourage you to press on to be all that God has called you to be. Let them remind you that God has plans to give you a future and a hope for your life and your marriage.[6] And, to remind you, as He did me, that with the faith of a mustard seed, we can move mountains and transform marriages.[7] If you are experiencing a dryness or brokenness in your marriage, read on. God has the recipe for a sweet, delicious marital relationship — a *Chocolate Cake Marriage*.

Two

What If We Believe?

*Despite all my emotions, I will hope in God again. I will believe and praise
the One who saves me and is my life, My Savior and my God*

- Psalm 43:5 VOICE

I pen this book with a unique perspective. I know what it's like to be married to an unbeliever, and I now know what it's like to be married to a believer. I experienced an extremely difficult first marriage wrought with infidelity, drugs, strife, and sorrow—my pillow was often wet with tears. The tears of sorrow have been replaced with tears of joy and laughter in my *last* marriage—with Christ at its center. Yet my marriage is not perfect. Every marriage requires work, discipline, and time on our knees in prayer. Most marriages have both times of hurt and times of delight. God has used both of my marriages to grow me into the woman He designed me to be. Keep in mind that every marriage is the perfect environment for sanctification.

Would you be willing to listen to my heart while reading these pages? To know that I am right there with you—learning and trying, attempting and failing—hungering for the abundant life God says we can have here on earth?

Like you, I have good days and bad days. Days when respecting my husband comes easily and naturally, and days when respect is the last thing I want to demonstrate. At times I'm sure I am on his last nerve and he is on mine. Some days the enemy of my soul whispers in my ear, "You should just give him a piece of your mind." Oh, how we need Jesus to help us be the women He has called us to be.

> *Like you, I have good days and bad days.*

Can we determine to take God's call on our lives seriously? Could we decide to go all in? I believe we can have marriages filled with love, joy, and passion. We can have marriages that reflect the incredible relationship that Christ has with His bride, the church. But we need to take a step of faith. That step of believing God is who He says He is and He will do what He says He will do! If we choose to trust God's promises and follow His recipe—the recipe He outlines for us in His Word— we can have different marriages than perhaps we do right now.

God's way can produce what I call a *Chocolate Cake Marriage*. God's word gives us distinct directions for marriage, and He says that He is for us and He wants to bless us. The creator of the universe really wants to bless us! Abundantly! But sometimes those blessings only come after obedience. The "if/thens" we see strategically placed throughout God's love letter to us are there to provoke action. If my people who are called by my name will humble themselves and seek My face, then I will heal their marriages.[8] (author's paraphrase) God is waiting for us to go all in, dear one.

We need to remind ourselves that all things work together and are fitting into a plan for good for those who love God and are called according to His design and purpose. [9] Our amazing, all-powerful Abba Father gives us that promise. Hold onto that truth, sweet sister, as you are led along the path God has before you. He will use each and every high and low for our ultimate good. Let's trust Him for that truth.

I am with you in this fight to have a marriage that is a joy to live in day in and day out—even on days when we find ourselves wondering why we said, "I do." We need to be aware that an enemy confronts us daily trying to steal, kill and destroy.[10] Victory is within reach with the right battle plan. Before we talk about what the plan looks like, or

> *We need to be aware that an enemy confronts us daily, trying to steal, kill and destroy.*

what I like to call God's recipe for a healthy marriage, let me give you a quick thumbnail sketch about Michelle Sullivan. Perhaps if you know my heart and a bit of my story, you might be more open to considering my advice and counsel as we start to apply the principles on these pages.

I came into this world in a hospital in Vancouver, British Columbia, Canada. My father worked for IBM—which stands for I'll Be Moving! We moved around quite a lot as I was growing up because Dad was promoted often, and with each promotion came relocation. We lived in Burnaby, North Vancouver, Toronto, New York, Calgary, back to Toronto, and then finally landed in West Vancouver to stay.

From the outside looking in, our family seemed quite typical. My younger brother, sister and I took piano lessons, ice skated at the park, and attended extracurricular activities after school. We did well in school and received awards for various accomplishments. Within our four walls, however, life was quite dysfunctional. From my viewpoint, my parents' marriage seemed cold and distant. I don't recall ever catching them share a passionate kiss or giggling with each other. As a young girl, I didn't find this strange as I didn't know things could, or even should, be different. Now as a grown woman experiencing a passionate and joy-filled marriage, I realize their relationship was broken.

My father committed adultery multiple times, and the coldness in their interactions spilled over into their relationships with my siblings and me. I often felt lonely in my own home and wished I had someone to talk to. Sometimes I would lie on my bed at night and pretend my Mom was sitting next to me, telling me stories and asking about my day.

We were not a church-going family. Although one day when filling out forms for school, I asked my Mom, "What religion are we?" I was simply told, "We are Protestants, dear." I checked that box not knowing a thing about what I had declared. My only recollection of hearing God's name spoken in our home was at Thanksgiving or Christmas when my Grandma or Grandpa said a blessing before our meal.

When I was fourteen years old, my dad took my brother, sister and me on an Easter vacation to Hawaii to break the news that he had decided to divorce our mother. The affairs and late nights at the country club had finally taken a toll on their fifteen-year marriage. I remember my dad asking what I thought about the decision, and my naïve, adolescent response in that surreal moment was, "I just want you and Mom to be happy."

I had no idea what a tidal wave of regrets, disappointments, and heartbreaks this decision would bring. To this very day, the scar of the disintegration of our family runs deep. This is why God hates divorce. He knows the pain it inflicts—not just on the immediate family, but for generations to come. My teenage years are mostly a blur of anguish and survival. Though my father told us of the impending divorce, he left unexpectedly. When he didn't come home one night, our mother had to explain that he had indeed moved out. When the messy divorce proceedings shifted into gear, my stay-at-home mom joined the workforce to attempt to build her own measure of financial security. Splintered lives and shifting sand tore a hole in our already shaky foundation.

When the cat's away, the mice will play. With no adult presence, our house quickly became the after school local teenage hang out. My friends and I stole menthol cigarettes from Mom's purse and pilfered my parents' liquor cabinet of Crème de Menthe and Grand Marnier. Alcohol became my drug of choice—all in an attempt to numb the pain I felt as I navigated the difficulties experienced by a hormonal adolescent suffering the disintegration of our family. My sister and I both lost our virginity in the downstairs family room in that house as the combination of booze and lack of supervision became a dreadful concoction.

After graduating from high school, I moved onto campus at the University of British Columbia. The drinking and partying continued, and one fateful night in 1983, my life's path took a fork in the road that started a long journey on a trail filled with potholes, sharp turns and dead ends. Friends and I decided to go to Whistler Mountain for a ski weekend during spring break. The beautiful resort of Blackcomb/Whistler was our local mountain—just an hour and a half from campus. We arrived as the Après Ski bars were opening. I was only eighteen, too young to get into a bar, but I had a newly acquired fake ID thanks to an advertisement on the back page of the *National Enquirer*. Perhaps somewhat prophetically, I selected a California driver's license. The card looked nothing like an actual California license, but it was laminated, so it must be real, right?

Continuing the California theme, I met a man that night who was from the Golden State. He spotted me across the smoky barroom and invited me to dance. I quickly accepted, and we headed to the dance floor to the beat of "Gloria" by Laura Branigan. I needed to slow down like the lyrics of the song suggested, but instead I got swept up in the excitement that an older man was interested in me. It simply felt nice to be noticed.

We drank and danced the night away, then exchanged phone numbers. After the tumultuous breakup of our family and the abandonment by my father, I enjoyed the attention of a man. When the nightclub closed, this California native invited me to his condo to relax in his Jacuzzi. I naively believed he simply wanted to take a dip in the hot tub. However, vanity came to the rescue to prevent a one-night-stand. I hadn't shaved in several days and was not about to put on a bathing suit and climb into a whirlpool with cactus legs! I declined the invitation, which he later shared, charmed him. Apparently, he wasn't used to rejection. He asked for my address and phone number which began our long-distance relationship of daily phone calls and a stack of handwritten letters.

After only a year of knowing each other—ninety-five percent spent with over a thousand miles between us—he asked me to marry him during a phone call on my twentieth birthday. I did not know the Lord, so it didn't don on me to even spend a minute in prayer about such a huge decision. Why would I say no to sunny beaches, Hollywood glamor, and Disneyland? As an added bonus, I liked the idea of escaping the pressures of university and my tumultuous family life—both my mom and dad had new companions, and I did not fit well into their new social lives. So, at the ripe old age of twenty years old, I said, "I do," and began a very long sojourn of loneliness, confusion and heartache. The problem with attempting to escape dysfunction is that your baggage tends to follow you on the voyage.

My new husband and I were both products of broken homes—his mother had been divorced twice and married three times—and we had both been deceived by the lie that drugs and alcohol provide an easy escape from the pain. What we didn't realize in our immaturity was that this counterfeit escape route was riddled with trapdoors and dead ends that led to more misery. Our home was often dotted with empty beer cans, smoking bongs, and small mirrors coated with residue left from snorted lines of cocaine. Often left alone on Friday nights while my then-husband went barhopping with his single friends, I had escaped one life of dysfunction only to land smack dab in the middle of another one. The honeymoon was over before it had begun.

Hindsight always seems 20/20, doesn't it? As a young woman, I had little reference or understanding of what life could be like or should be like. In the midst of the turmoil of those early years of marriage, life felt strangely normal. The same feelings of isolation, loneliness and emptiness that I had growing up had stowed away with me on the trip to California and settled in nicely to their new address.

Meanwhile, back in Canada, a female acquaintance of my father invited him to a Billy Graham crusade. With no real excuse to say no, he accepted simply because this woman needed an escort and the date was open on his calendar. Raised in a home where faithfulness and joy were not modeled, my dad was also a product of brokenness. So intrigued by what he heard from Mr. Graham's pulpit that spring night in 1984, my dad decided to go back the following evening by himself. During that second night, the Word of God softened my dad's hardened heart, and when the invitation was given, he went forward and accepted Jesus as his Lord and Savior.

Soon afterward, my dad wanted to share his new faith with his newlywed daughter. However, he came on a bit too strong for me with a "turn or burn" message of fire and brimstone. He tried to point out the drug and alcohol use in my life that were masquerading as peacemakers when in fact they were pain creators. He tried to convince us that pot and piná coladas were leading us down an empty path, and Jesus was the only One who could truly bring fulfillment and purpose coupled with the provision of peace.

At the time, it seemed hypocritical for my father to point his finger at us, describing our life as sinful, when in my eyes, he had modeled that lifestyle during my most formative years. His long letters urging repentance made their way into the circular file in our home—tossed in the trash with a roll of the eyes. Next, he'll be holding up John 3:16 signs at football games, I thought to myself.

After a successful career with IBM, my dad ventured into multi-level marketing—seemingly always peddling the latest get-rich-quick scheme. "You just need to buy in and start your own downline," was a common mantra. I concluded that his new religion was just another one of those campaigns that would cost me in the end. He had tried to sell me on Jojoba Beans, Melaleuca, Amway, and JewelWay. This seemed like "JesusWay," and I wasn't buying.

Several years went by, and the newlyweds put up enough walls that the Jesus letters stopped coming. However, when we went to Vancouver to visit my dad and his new wife in 1986, I noticed a few changes in my father. He had a tenderness and a peace I had never witnessed before in him. I was intrigued.

Some months went by, and my husband and I decided what our rocky marriage needed wasn't Jesus. We needed a baby! It took us almost a year to conceive, but almost four years to the day of our wedding, our first son, Steven, was born. With great excitement, my dad flew to California to meet his first grandson and during that visit, I asked my dad about his new faith.

"I like the changes I've seen in you, Dad," I said. "I would like the peace and joy that you have. How can I join the club? Is there a membership card? Are there dues to pay? A downline to create? Or, perhaps a visitation by an angel? Tell me how to join."

My dad smiled and carefully pulled a well-worn piece of paper out of his wallet—this is a photo of the actual note :

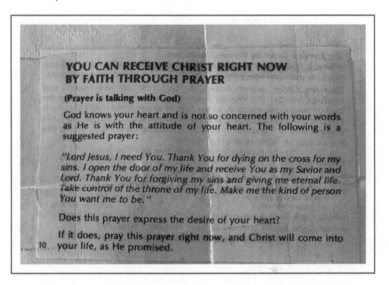

Accepting Jesus wasn't about joining a religion or paying dues like I assumed. Becoming a Christian wasn't about going to church, or reciting Bible passages. And being born again wasn't about trying to be a better person. Salvation was about a relationship with God. Believing that I was a sinner who needed a savior and repenting of my sins. Trusting that Jesus died on the cross to save me from my sin. That His blood paid the price for all my iniquities, past, present and future, casting them as far as the east is from the west.[11] And to prove who He is, Jesus rose again from the dead so that whoever believes in Him shall not perish but have eternal life.[12]

I would like the peace and joy that you have.

My dad pointed out that all the other gods and gurus of other religions are still in the grave: Muhammad, Buddha, Joseph Smith, Confucius, Darwin, Steven Hawking, Mary Baker Eddy, etc. Jesus conquered death as a sign that He is God who was, and is, and is to come.[13]

I believed in my heart that night and asked Jesus to come into my life and be my Lord and Savior.

That was Thanksgiving Eve of 1988, and my life changed dramatically since that day. Peace flooded my heart, coupled with a desire to read my Bible and seek God's will for my life. And, I actually looked forward to going to church that weekend. I experienced the same peace and joy I saw in my Dad. I was born again.[14]

Challenge

Have you committed your life to Jesus Christ? All throughout Scripture, we are told that He is the way, the truth and the life. There is no other way to heaven except through faith in the death and resurrection of Jesus. The Word became flesh,[15] went to the cross and shed His blood in order to remove our sins as far as the east is from the west.[16] He suffered the penalty of sin for us so that we can enjoy abundant life on earth and eternity in heaven in the presence of a Holy God. Now that's good news. Would you consider dedicating or re-dedicating your life to Him right now? He can be the difference between having a marriage on the rocks and one built on The Rock.

Three

Is She Divorced?

"For I hate divorce!" says the Lord, the God of Israel. "To divorce your wife is to overwhelm her with cruelty," says the Lord of Heaven's Armies. "So guard your heart; do not be unfaithful to your wife."

-Malachi 2:16

God hates divorce. We should hate divorce too. Sometimes separation and divorce enter lives outside our control. My first husband did not share the same passion or desire to know God that I did. Though he attended church services on occasion, he did not want a Savior, let alone a Lord. Our passions and desires began to clash.

The Bible refers to the marriage of a believer to an unbeliever as "unequally yoked." My husband still liked smoking pot, snorting cocaine, and viewing pornography—and, quite frankly, he wondered where the woman who used to clean his bong for him had gone. My predicament was difficult. However, the Bible is very clear that if you are married to an unbeliever, if he is willing to stay in the marriage, you should stay and love your husband.

And if a believing woman has a husband who is not a believer and

he is willing to continue living with her, she must not leave him.

For the believing wife brings holiness to her marriage.

- I Corinthians 7:13-14a

I needed to learn how to love him in a way that would not make him feel like Jesus was the new man in my life. At this point, I had a lot to learn.

We went on to have three more sons, Shane, Tanner and JP—four boys in less than seven years. Raising boys while unequally yoked proved to be increasingly difficult. As co-parents, we each had a different agenda as to what we wanted to instill in our children. I wanted our sons to love God with all their hearts, souls and minds. Their dad had another plan, and our priorities often conflicted. He was a good father in many ways, but he did not want to *train up a child in the way he should go.*[17]

Encountering life's trials became more arduous because the man I married did not believe in the power of prayer, nor in seeking God for wisdom. I often felt alone and yearned to lean on my husband for spiritual support. For example, when our oldest son, Steven, was ten years old, he contracted an unusual strain of meningitis. Placed in isolation in Children's Hospital of Orange County, Steven was visited a number of times by a physician from the Centers of Disease Control who explained that our son was very sick. The doctors struggled to determine a plan of action. I remember pacing the halls of the hospital and feeling so alone. Stranded on a spiritual island, I could not reach for my husband's hand to pray.

Several years later, Tanner began to have daily grand mal seizures, and

doctors recommended we have half his brain surgically removed. Yes, half.
Storming the gates of heaven in prayer as a couple would have been so com-
forting and reassuring. However, though that did not happen, Jesus was always
by my side, and He was my comforter during that trial. My job was to be the salt
and light to those around me, including my husband. I failed often and learned
many lessons the hard way, but God held my hand and taught me along the
way.

One of the most difficult aspects of our unequally yoked marriage was
that my home was not my sanctuary. Ideally, we should find peace, encouragement, and fellowship within the walls of our dwellings; however, in my case, and
perhaps this is true for you too, our home was often filled with strife, arguments,
and discouragement. Thankfully, we are never alone when we know Jesus. God
continued to speak truth to my heart, and He was my sustainer and my guide.

In the same way, wives, you should patiently accept the authority

of your husbands. This is so that even if they don't obey God's word, as they

observe your pure respectful behavior, they may be persuaded without a

word by the way you live.

- 1 Peter 3:1-2 VOICE

Only beginning to learn to trust God and to read His word each day,
initially my behavior was far from wholesome and respectful. I made so many
mistakes as a baby Christian struggling in a rocky marriage. I hated observing
the boys' dad model the opposite of what I wanted for our sons—sadly, my re-
actions to his sinful behaviors were often equally sinful. Unintentionally, I taught
our sons disrespect, when I demonstrated disrespect to their father. I needed to

seek God for wisdom and direction rather than nagging my husband to change. Learn from my mistake, sweet sister, and don't attempt to be your husband's Holy Spirit.

Those difficult years in my marriage laid the foundation for my deep reliance and trust in God. The disorder in my life finally brought me to my knees— right where I should have gone in the first place. I learned to seek my Father in heaven, fall on my face before Him, and tap into His limitless fountain of strength and peace. God knew there were changes that needed to be made in my unbelieving husband, but there were changes to be made in my heart as well. God allowed me to walk through a dark, pain-filled valley to bring me to a place where I could finally say, "It is well with my soul." When Jesus is all you have, you realize that Jesus is all you need.

> *I needed to seek God for wisdom and direction rather than nagging my husband to change.*

Certain situations pressed me closer to Jesus than others. Despite the breadcrumbs that led to the door of proven adultery, the boys' dad always denied any infidelity. He told me that he loved me too much to be unfaithful. When I asked him about a phone number scrawled on the inside of a matchbook cover in his pocket, or why he was hours late coming home from the golf course, he would tell me to stop making mountains out of molehills.

Then there came an afternoon I will never forget. He had returned from one of his many business trips to Asia and was sharing all he had done on his three-week tour. He pulled out his camera to show me some pictures— images of tall, picturesque buildings, stunning skylines, and beautiful smiles on the Asian faces. Then he scrolled to a picture that stopped my heart—a young Chinese woman posed for the camera sitting on a bed in a negligée.

"Who is this?!" I demanded. Stammering, he answered, "Uh, uh, I don't know who that is. Someone else must have used my camera." Right before my eyes, the molehill morphed into a mountain.

At this point, I had been a Christian for almost fifteen years and believed that everything allowed into my life was Father-filtered. Many times, I reacted to my husband's sin with sin of my own. In this instance, I determined to wait on the Lord and let my response be tempered by His Spirit. I cried out for wisdom and strength as I did not want to react in my flesh and live to regret it. Everything in me wanted to smash the camera on the ground and pound my husband's chest. God is so faithful to never leave us or forsake us.[18] He gave me immediate strength and peace as I shot a prayer to Him as to what I should do in that moment. Ask and it will be given to you.[19] We just need to take the time to ask. And then be still and wait for the answer. Not always easy, but with God all things are truly possible. We just need to be careful to not step into the trap that Satan puts on our path.

> *Many times, I reacted to my husband's sin with sin of my own.*

My husband moved toward me "to explain," but I put my hand up as I pushed past him, grabbed my purse, and walked out the front door. I jumped in my car, managed to get the key in the ignition, and pulled out of the driveway with no idea where to go. Surprisingly, I was not crying as I drove and drove and drove. Eventually, I parked beneath a tree at a park where the boys often played their Little League games. Opening the Bible that I kept in my car, the Lord led me to several passages, all which brought great comfort and calm to my heart. Then God made it crystal clear that I needed to ask my husband for a time of separation. In our marriage vows, we professed that we would be faithful until death do us part, and he obviously did not stick to that pledge.

Our separation was surreal. Rather than traveling as a family to our boys' soccer games and tennis matches, we traveled from separate homes in separate cars. We avoided each other on the sidelines while shooting the occasional glance. Unfair. That is the word that taunted me. Why was I forced onto this path of irreconcilable differences when I was faithful to our vows to forsake all others? Why did I have to endure the look of pain on our boys' faces?

After a couple of weeks, he invited me to dinner, presented me with a dozen roses, apologized, and told me he wanted to come home. The separation was hard on our boys, so my mother's heart leaned hard toward allowing him to return. Plus, doesn't God tell us to forgive? Seventy times seven?[20] He did seem sincerely sorry and repentant. Yes, we are to forgive, but we are also to be still and know that He is God and *wait* for Him to direct our steps.[21] I made a huge mistake right at this point. Feelings overtook wisdom in the race to resolution, and a price was paid because I did not wait on the Lord for confirmation that this was His timing for reconciliation.

My husband came back into our home before he had truly sought the Lord for restoration and healing of his own soul. The first month after he returned, everything seemed fine. He went to see our pastor for counseling, we attended church as a family, and he even agreed to join a neighborhood couples' Bible study focused on marriage. However, the evening of the first meeting, he decided he didn't want to go. Old behaviors returned, and we were right back in the rut.

Several months later, a technician came to our home to fix our internet. My husband was at work, but his computer sat on the kitchen island. The technician needed to inspect all our laptops to make sure he had resolved the issue. When I logged onto my husband's computer, an unread email appeared on the screen. The subject line read, "Your eCard has been received."

ECard? He doesn't send eCards.

As the young technician worked on our modem, I focused on uncovering the recipient and nature of the card. My heart stopped when I clicked on the link. The card was sexual in content and was addressed to another woman stating he missed her smile and he looked forward to seeing her soon—another stab to my numb heart. I gave an Academy Award-winning performance as I hid my racing heart from the tech and my sons, who were playing billiards in the same room.

After the technician left, I went upstairs and sobbed into my pillow. "I can't do this anymore, Lord. I can't stay with a man who says, 'I love you and don't want to lose you' one minute but has relationships that speak the opposite. I believe I can do all things through You. But I just can't live this anymore."

I soon discovered I was married to a serial adulterer. The Lord revealed to me through a series of events that only God could unfold that the boys' father was not merely unfaithful through pornographic internet exchanges and naked massages, but my husband of twenty-four years was in a relationship with a woman in another state and had multiple liaisons in Asia where he traveled for business.

Strength, strength, Lord. I need Your strength. I need Your wisdom and Your peace. My world is crashing around me. I felt betrayed, angry, disappointed, used, and numb all at the same time.

I asked for another separation. The boy's father refused counseling and had no repentance about the adultery. Nevertheless, the day he moved out, he sent me a text that read, "Miss you already." I pressed on in God's strength, raising the four boys virtually on my own at that point as their father only saw them a handful of times during the first few months of our separation.

My heart reeled from the pain and anxiety that my circumstances brought. A host of other difficult situations occurred—my oldest son witnessed a murder in our quiet neighborhood. My second son required emergency surgery. Our third son ran away from home due to the turmoil. My stepfather was diagnosed with cancer, etc., etc. Life does go on.

I needed God's help so desperately. I had never experienced anxiety attacks before, but they became a reality during this time of transition from "dual parents, family of six" to "single-mom, family of five." Feeling my heart suddenly race and panic set in was very unfamiliar—normally I handled crisis well. In the darkness and dryness of that particular valley, unrest crept in. I clung to God and pressed into every word of wisdom He had for me. I thirsted for His Word and His counsel. God, how can I survive this? As I sought Him, He was always faithful to provide me the guidance and the strength I needed.

> *I pray that from his glorious, unlimited resources he will*
> *empower you with inner strength through his Spirit.*
> - Ephesians 3:16

> *Then call on me when you are in trouble,*
> *and I will rescue you, and you will give me glory.*
> - Psalm 50:15

Wanting to make sure I had not contracted an STD from his extramarital affairs, I went for a physical, and a rush of humiliation and shame flooded my heart as I entered the physician's office. Again, why did I have to go through this when I had remained faithful? The doctor ushered me into the small examination room and asked how I was doing emotionally, and she pressed to write a prescription for anti-anxiety medication. Even after I told her that I was going to rely on the Lord to give me peace, she stuck the prescription pad out and said, "This will help." I am not against medications and would never urge anyone to get off something prescribed by their doctor. However, I do believe our society is too quick to medicate away feelings we would rather not experience—emotions that God might use to bring us closer to Him, instead of to a pharmacy. God is our peace and will pull us up and out of the mire as we turn to Him. He eventually took away all my anxiety.

> *He reached down and drew me from the deep, dark hole where I was stranded, mired in the muck and clay. With a gentle hand, He pulled me out to set me down safely on a warm rock; He held me until I was steady enough to continue the journey again.*
>
> *- Psalm 40:2 VOICE*

God hates divorce, so I prayed for restoration. How could I speak to women about marriage if my own was failing? However, my husband had no desire to repent. Nor did the woman he was having an affair with as I wrote a letter to her reminding her that she was involved with a married man. I encouraged her to seek the Lord, ask for forgiveness and that His grace was available to her as well. However, the affair continued. God reminded me that though He hates divorce, He hates adultery, too. After twenty-five years of marriage, eighteen months of separation, four amazing sons, lots of highs and many lows, we were granted a divorce. The California courts do not allow adultery as grounds for divorce, so we joined the statistics of failed marriages due to "irreconcilable differences."

I pen this book as a woman who has known the heartache of divorce—something I would not wish on my worst enemy. There is a reason God hates divorce, for it is a horrid, painful, lonely experience. However, I also now know the true meaning of how God can restore the years the locusts have eaten.[22] Less than a year after the divorce, the Lord brought a wonderful man into my life—a godly man who loves the Lord and cherishes me. I will tell you more about him in another chapter, but suffice it to say, God has truly allowed me to exchange my ashes for beauty.[23]

> I pen this book as a woman who has known the heartache of divorce.

In these pages, I share nuggets of wisdom I learned from my marriage to an unbeliever. There are also many lessons God has taught me while married to a believer. Marriage is work—whether you are married to a guy who lies on the couch with a six-pack of beer and plays video games all day or you are married to a man who sings on the worship team and brings you breakfast in bed on Saturday mornings.

Marriage is not easy. God created this union of two sinners who are wired completely different, who often have dissimilar interests, personalities, vocabularies and sex drives, and they are asked to live together harmoniously until death do they part. Talk about a recipe for disaster. Even when Adam and Eve first ate of the fruit of the tree of knowledge of good and evil, God told Adam, "And I will cause hostility between you and the woman." [24] Yikes! But God, in His infinite wisdom, has an amazing plan for us through the covenant of marriage—to learn to die to self, to love unconditionally, and to serve one another. I'm excited to go on this journey with you because our good Shepherd has a beautiful plan to lead us and guide us each step of the way. We do not head out on this path alone—Jesus will light the way. He has a good plan for you, one that includes a future and a hope[25]—don't let anyone tell you otherwise.

My heart's desire is to share some of what God has shown me through trusting Him, seeking His face, and finding the peace that He promises. Our dear Abba Father says He will keep in perfect peace all those who trust in Him, whose thoughts are fixed on Him.[26] We just have to trust that God will do what He says He will do, and that we can do all things through Christ who strengthens us![27] Amen?

To help us make real changes, I provide you with a challenge at the end of each chapter. Some are simple and merely require jotting down a thought or memorizing a verse. A few might require folding your hands in prayer before attempting. Remember, if we want to see changes in our marriages, we need to make changes—to actually *do* things differently. I've heard it said that the definition of insanity is to continue to do the same thing and expect a different outcome. We can be women who influence change, but we have to decide to *want* that change. Perhaps these chapter challenges will be the tool to help you make a few modifications. I hope you decide to go all in and determine to start today to be a woman of influence and a woman who will stop at nothing in order to protect her marriage and her family.

> *We just have to trust that God will do what He says He will do, and that we can do all things through Christ who strengthens us.*

Take a few moments to write out 1 Corinthians 13:4-7, perhaps on a 3x5 card or into the notes section of your phone. Commit this verse to memory. If we would simply live out this verse, 90 percent of our marriage difficulties would fade away.

Love is very patient and kind, never jealous or envious, never boastful or proud, never haughty or selfish or rude. Love does not demand its own way. It is not irritable or touchy. It does not hold grudges and will hardly even notice when others do it wrong. It is never glad about injustice, but rejoices whenever truth wins out. If you love someone, you will be loyal to him no matter what the cost. You will always believe in him, always expect the best of him, and always stand your ground in defending him.

- 1 Corinthians 13:4-7 TLB

Practice each line by asking yourself:

- *How can I better respond to my husband when he behaves poorly?*
- *How can I model love even when I feel like giving up?*
- *Who can I ask to pray for me and my marriage?*

Write down the answers to these questions as pen to paper starts you on a path of completion and resolution.

Four

What's Your Exchange Policy?

I am my beloved's and my beloved is mine.

-Song of Solomon 6:3a TLB

S ome items we buy in the marketplace come with the policy "No Exchanges, No Returns"— bathing suits, pillows, perishables, and sale items to name a few. God wants us to apply this policy to our husbands too. No exchanges, no returns.

Misconceptions abound when it comes to the topics of separation and divorce, so I'd like to clear the fog in regard to these touchy subjects. Biblically, I believe there are only two main conditions deemed reasonable circumstances for divorce if you are a follower of Christ. The first scenario is if a believer is married to an unbeliever, and the unbelieving spouse abandons his family. Bags are packed, the car is loaded, and there is no forwarding address. The believer is left with very few options, and one option could be divorce. The Lord allows her to move on with her life, and a divorce might be part of that process.

But if the husband or wife who isn't a believer insists on leaving, let them go.

In such cases the believing husband or wife is no longer bound to the other,

for God has called you to live in peace.

- 1 Corinthians 7:15

The second and only other biblical justification for divorce is adultery.

Jesus said, "Moses provided for divorce as a concession to your hard heart-

edness, but it is not part of God's original plan. I'm holding you to the original

plan, and holding you liable for adultery if you divorce your faithful wife and

then marry someone else. I make an exception in cases where the spouse

has committed adultery."

- Matthew 19:8-9 MSG

The legal definition of adultery is: Voluntary sexual intercourse between a married person and another person who is not their married spouse.[28]

Unfaithfulness is not always the kiss of death to a marital relationship. Many marriages survive and even flourish post-adultery when true repentance and forgiveness takes place. Several dear friends whose husbands were unfaithful enjoyed remarkable reconciliation when mercy trumped divorce through the power of the Holy Spirit. They have some of the strongest marriages I've witnessed because they fought long and hard for them. Saying it is not easy to live with someone who committed adultery is an understatement, but with God anything is possible.[29] Their marriages became stronger through the storm. Like trees on top of a hill that have borne the brunt of gale force winds for years—they become stronger and more valuable. Their trunks are the strongest and their wood most useful because of the storms they've weathered.

My brave friends' desire to forgive and their toil for restoration occurred in part because they shared an awareness that God hates divorce. They wanted to do everything possible to avoid something God hates.

> *"For I hate divorce!" says the Lord, the God of Israel. "To divorce your wife is to overwhelm her with cruelty," says the Lord of Heaven's Armies. "So, guard your heart; do not be unfaithful to your wife."*
>
> - Malachi 2:16

With the biblical boundaries for divorce set in place, an interesting statistic from one survey showed that only one in seven divorces (fourteen percent) were granted due to adultery.[30] Less than one percent of divorces were granted because of desertion. If these statistics hold true, about eighty-five percent of divorces are *unbiblical* and should not have been filed if a Christian was involved. If we want to see healing in our homes and in our land, we need to get serious about obeying God and His Word.

> *Then if my people who are called by my name will humble themselves and pray and seek my face and turn from their wicked ways, I will hear from heaven and will forgive their sins and restore their land.*
>
> - 2 Chronicles 7:14

The legal mumbo jumbo in most of America today is that sufficient grounds for divorce apply if you and your spouse don't get along any more or don't have anything in common. Those are far from adequate grounds if you're a believer in Jesus Christ. What we have in common with our spouses are the vows we made before God to love one another until death do us part—even if that has become the only thing we have in common. God commands that what He brings together let man not separate.[31] Let's determine to take this seriously no matter how difficult the path. I can vouch from my own experience that I forgave my first husband multiple times for unfaithfulness before finally feeling that separation and divorce were my only option for health and safety reasons. But that was a last resort. I did everything I could to be obedient to God and His Word, including forgiving seventy times seven.[32]

If the enemy whispers in your ear that God wants you to be happy and you shouldn't have to put up with "Fred" anymore, that is truly a lie from the pit of hell. Combat the lie with truth. God might be using an arduous situation in your marriage as the catalyst for a closer walk with Him. My first marriage pressed me into the arms of my Heavenly Father like nothing before. I had no other means to get through that difficult valley than to seek the Lord for strength and peace.

The Lord gives his people strength. The Lord blesses them with peace.

- Psalm 29:11

Ask yourself if you are willing to trust God with your marriage. Are you truly dedicated to opening His manual and following it no matter how difficult the instructions might be? God longs for us to have healthy marriages, but He needs our cooperation to make the necessary changes. He will not storm in and make robots out of us. He will not wave a magic wand to make us honor and obey 'til death do us part. He wants His daughters to seek His face and obey—and leave the rest to our Abba Father.

> *Do you think all God wants are sacrifices—empty rituals just for show?*
> *He wants you to listen to him! Plain listening is the thing,*
> *not staging a lavish religious production. Not doing*
> *what God tells you is far worse than fooling around in the occult.*
> - 1 Samuel 15:22-23a MSG

We need to be willing to obey God which means obeying everything in His Word.

God tells us in Psalm 37:4 (NASB): *Delight yourself in the Lord; and He will give you the desires of your heart.* If the desire of your heart is to have a blessed marriage, then ask yourself, "Am I delighting in the Lord?" Am I putting Him

We need to be willing to obey God

first in my life, meditating on His Word, seeking His direction, and obeying His instructions? The order is very clear. First, delight in Him and *then* He will give us the desires of our hearts. Only you know if this is true in your world. If delighting in the Lord is not something you do, begin today and He will give you the desires of your heart in His perfect timing. Will you trust Him? Immanuel, God with us, is ready and willing to take your hand and walk you step by step.

Challenge

Write Psalm 37:4 on a 3x5 card, and put it where you will see it often. Commit this verse to memory, and you will find yourself thinking less and less about an exchange or return for the man God blessed you with.

Delight yourself in the Lord; and He will give you the desires of your heart.

- Psalm 37:4 NASB

Five

Lord, Fix My Husband!

When all this transpires, you will finally have the answers you have been seeking. I tell you the truth, anything you ask of the Father in My name, He will give to you. Until this moment, you have not sought after anything in My name. Ask and you will receive so that you will be filled with joy.

-John 16:23b VOICE

efore the adultery and the divorce, my first marriage lacked joy and peace, and plain old frustration reigned. The relationship was void of passion and romance as numbness settled in and made itself at home. Exhausted by the struggle and beginning to lose hope that anything would ever change, I called out to God. Unfortunately, my initial expectation was that God would change my husband. After all, using drugs, avoiding church and failing to model good manners were on his list of character flaws—not mine. He must be the hitch in this relationship. Based on that assumption, my prayers often sounded like this:

"God, *fix my husband*. Do a work in him, Lord! That's what our marriage needs—a husband makeover. Change him, God, please! Make him understand me, encourage me, support me, appreciate me, hug me, hold me, need me, want me. Oh, and if he could bring me flowers and not leave his wet towel on the floor, that would be great, too. Then, I know we will be happy. *Then*, I can be a good wife. *Then,* my joy will most surely be complete. Thank you, Lord. In Your Name I pray, Amen."

There, that should do it. God said to ask, so I asked. I'll just keep praying until God fixes my husband, and *then* things will be better. Have you ever felt that way? That God simply needs to transform your husband and *then* you can endeavor to move from roommate to soul mate?

If we desire change in our marriage, yet we go into our prayer closet with the notion that it is only our husband who requires the makeover, we are going about change the wrong way. God desires transformation in our husband, *and* in us too. In my first marriage, I wearied of adapting to my husband's shortcomings and felt I had made plenty of changes and compromises. After all, I read the books on marriage, put up with his drug use, and tried to overlook most of his other faults. That's change, isn't it? What more was I supposed to do?

Somehow, I had been convinced that simply putting up with his bad behaviors and poor habits was above and beyond doing my part to help our marriage. I was already a good wife, right? Perhaps. I did some things right, but I avoided looking in the mirror and asking God to change me. God had a

> *I avoided looking in the mirror and asking God to change me.*

makeover in mind for Michelle as well. An Extreme Spouse Makeover. It took far too many strife-filled nights sleeping in separate rooms before I came to the realization that we both needed renovating by the right Designer. God is ready and waiting to enter the doors of our marriages to start the remodel process if we are willing. God will not bust the door down and make us do what is best. We have to give Him the keys and let Him in. Once we allow Him access, He simply needs our obedience and the makeover begins. We have an audience of One, and we fool ourselves if we think we don't have to obey Him just because our spouse isn't.

> *"What is more pleasing to the Lord: your burnt offerings and sacrifice or your obedience to his voice? Listen! Obedience is better than sacrifice, and submission is better than offering the fat of rams."*
>
> - 1 Samuel 15:22

> *And this is love: that we walk in obedience to his commands. As you have heard from the beginning, his command is that you walk in love.*
>
> - 2 John 1:6 NIV

Would you like a happy, joy-filled marriage? Would you exchange a marriage rating of a "2" or even a "6" for one around an "8 ½"? Do you want to experience the same passion you did when you first got married? Of course. Sign us all up for that today, right? Can following God's ways really change things? Can we really trade in a mound of strife for a heap of peace? Absolutely! But, are we willing to do what God might ask us to do to affect change? God talks about wanting to give us an abundant life; however, how badly do we want it? What are we willing to do to achieve it?

Ask yourself this serious question: "Am I willing to seek my Father in Heaven, receive His instructions, and obey what He asks me to do so that I can have a more joy-filled marital relationship?" If I want my marriage to get well, am I willing to do whatever He asks to achieve the healing? The choice is real.

For too many years, I allowed myself to stay late at the pity party I was throwing for myself. Initially, I was not willing to make any changes because it seemed so hopeless. The rut was deep, the pain was real, and I didn't see a way out.

Do you remember the story from the book of John about the man who remained crippled for thirty-eight years? He was hanging out by the Pool of Bethesda located on the eastern side of Jerusalem— its water source coming from a nearby spring, with five porches similar to alcoves or doorways.

Crowds of people lined the area, lying around the porches. All of these people were disabled in some way; some were blind, lame, paralyzed, or plagued by diseases; and they were waiting for the waters to move. From time to time, a heavenly messenger would come to stir the water in the pool. Whoever reached the water first and got in after it was agitated would be healed of his or her disease.

- John 5:3-4 VOICE

When Jesus saw the crippled man lying on the porch amongst all the other blind, lame and paralyzed individuals, our Lord approached the man and asked him, "Would you like to get well?"[33] The question itself seems absurd since we know this man had suffered immobility for decades. Of course, he wanted to get well, right? He had been paralyzed and completely dependent on others for almost forty years. Can you imagine the discomfort, the bedsores, the filth, and the lack of freedom he must have endured? Every day, he would wait by the pool of water in the hope that somehow, he could get down to it in time to receive healing. I can't imagine waiting thirty-eight *days* lying on the ground hoping for healing, let alone thirty-eight *years*.

Thirty-eight years is about 14,000 sunrises and sunsets of sitting and waiting for healing with apparently no other purpose in life. How could Jesus ask him *if* he wanted healing? Wouldn't this man be willing to do *whatever* it took to pick up his mat and walk? To experience the freedom movement would provide? Or would he? The man's response is curious. Rather than responding, "Yes, yes, I want to be healed!" this crippled human replied, "Sir, I have no one to help me into the pool when the water is stirred. While I am trying to get in, someone else goes down ahead of me." Then Jesus said to him, "Get up! Pick up your mat and walk." At once the man was cured; he picked up his mat and walked.[34]

Sadly, I resembled that poor, crippled man—sitting around, waiting for someone else to "fix" the situation. Enduring the pain and pointing at others to explain why he was not healed—and yet longing for circumstances to change. If only "someone" would carry me to the water when it moves, there could be restoration. I suffered in pain and pointed at my husband to explain the lack of healing. But Jesus does not want us pointing to something or someone else. Jesus will bring healing when we are willing to obey Him. We don't need someone to take us anywhere. We need to be willing to take up our mat and walk. The question is, "Are we willing?" It will be up to you, sweet sister, to decide if you are up for the challenge. Perhaps, like me, you need to soften your heart, slowly uncross your arms, and say "I'm picking up my mat today. I'm ready to follow Jesus."

> *Jesus will bring healing when we are willing to obey Him.*

Oh, the joy that dear brother must have experienced. The previously crippled man later testifies to the Jewish leaders that someone healed him *and* gave him back his strength. Are you ready for healing and strengthening? Then you must simply submit yourself to God's instructions, even if they don't always make sense. Imagine how "Stand up, pick up your mat, and walk!" would have sounded to a crippled man. And, yet, the man was willing, so he was healed.

> *God has our absolute best interest in mind.*

How many of us might have simply said, "I can't"? Especially if we have faced the same difficulty for a long time. You might be thinking, "I can't follow what God says to do. I just can't." "My husband does not even deserve my respect and I'm tired of making a solo effort." "He never helps around the house, he never encourages me, and don't get me started on his habits and how he's hurt me."

Then, dear one, you might never see the healing. And you will remain paralyzed next to the pool of living water. Why not be keen to do what God asks and watch Him pour out His healing and His strength as only God can do? For the healing to happen, we have to be willing. Join me in a decision to say "yes" to Jesus.

He is our Creator and knows exactly what actions we need to take for the recovery in our marriage to begin. When He asks, "Do you want to get well?" don't respond with excuses. Instead, be ready to do what He asks you to do, and the healing and strength will come. God wants to bless you abundantly, sweet sister, but He does ask for our obedience. His love is unconditional, but many of His promises are conditional.

God has our absolute best interest in mind. He even has a strategy to prosper us and not cause us harm.

> *I know what I'm doing. I have it all planned out—plans to take care of you,*
> *not abandon you, plans to give you the future you hope for.*
> - Jeremiah 29:11 MSG

"But, Lord, my husband is the one You need to modify. He's the problem. He's the insensitive one. I am a good wife, overall. I do so much around here already. Why do I have to make more changes?"

That response is similar to the one given by the man lying paralyzed on the ground—it's an excuse. An excuse I muttered many times myself. But when God asks if we want healing, listen to what He tells us next. Don't be like the crippled man who was quick to blame his lack of healing on others.

> *But don't just listen to God's word. You must do what it says. Otherwise, you are only fooling yourselves. For if you listen to the word and don't obey, it is like glancing at your face in a mirror. You see yourself, walk away, and forget what you look like. But if you look carefully into the perfect law that sets you free, and if you do what it says and don't forget what you heard, then God will bless you for doing it.*
>
> *- James 1:22-25*

She will be blessed in what she does. What a promise. Do you want to be blessed? Then be a doer of God's word no matter what He asks you to do. Take up your mat and walk! Jeremiah continues God's instruction with this ...

> *"When you call on me, when you come and pray to me, I'll listen. When you come looking for me, you'll find me. Yes, when you get serious about finding me and want it more than anything else, I'll make sure you won't be disappointed." God's Decree. "I'll turn things around for you."*
>
> *- Jeremiah 29:12-14a MSG*

Early in my first marriage, I would pour my heart out to God, begging for restoration, reconciliation, and a resurrection of love in our relationship. However, I did not recognize that part of our problem was my unwillingness to unreservedly obey God and His commands. This reluctance delayed some of the healing that might have taken place.

Are you willing to join me in holding up the mirror? Take a peek at ourselves for a moment and let God give us the makeover He so desires to provide. Start today to truly be a doer of His word—not just a hearer. There are way too many hearers out there sitting around crippled by the poolside, but where are the doers? The ones who will pick up the mat? Let's determine to be women who believe our God because that is where strength and healing meet joy and blessings. God says we can do all things through Him. And, not only that, He will work all the things that are going on in our marriage for good, if we love Him and are called according to His purpose.[35]

Never forget that God is sovereign and knows exactly what is going on inside your four walls. He has not been caught off guard by what is happening in your relationship. He will use all the scenarios you are facing today to work out what is best for you and your husband—even, perhaps, by placing this book in your hands. Our Wonderful Father in heaven has a plan. He wrote the recipe for the healing. Don't be fooled into thinking that He doesn't know your situation, or that He doesn't care.

Notice God doesn't say He works *some* things for good, or *most* things, or even works *the good* things for good. Our Abba Father will work *ALL* things *for the good* of those who love Him. Will you decide with me today that you will honor and obey God and His perfect will for your life and your marriage?

The delightful truth is that God does not call us to do something that He will not then help us to accomplish. He has given us the recipe for marriage in His Word and the Holy Spirit to guide us in power.

Here's the knowledge you need: you will receive power

when the Holy Spirit comes on you.

- Acts 1:8 VOICE

We must *trust* Him and His timing, and He will take care of the details. He will also give you the strength to follow His directions.

I pray that God, the source of all hope, will infuse your lives with

an abundance of joy and peace in the midst of your faith so that your

hope will overflow through the power of the Holy Spirit.

- Romans 15:13 VOICE

Do you want to overflow with hope, sweet sister? It is ours for the asking.

Keep in mind that oftentimes obeying God requires waiting for the Lord to work things out in *His* timing and in *His* way. Humans so easily grow impatient. I know from experience. We want the microwave recipe, not the crockpot recipe, so we find ourselves "helping" God out a little to speed things up, only to find ourselves doing things in our marriage that end up delaying God's plan of restoration. Trust that He will work all that you are going through into His plan. He made you, and He allowed you to stand before witnesses in order to

> *The delightful truth is that God does not call us to do something that He will not then help us to accomplish.*

make vows to each other, 'til death do us part.

> *A man who makes a vow to the Lord or makes a pledge under oath must*
> *never break it. He must do exactly what he said he would do.*
> - Numbers 30:2

So unless your marriage vows included, "I take you, Fred, to be my husband, to have and to hold from this day forward, for better, for worse, for richer, for poorer, in sickness and in health, to love and to cherish 'til death do us part—unless I tire of you in between that time, and you begin to annoy me and leave your clothes on the floor and watch too much TV, play too many video games, belch and pass gas too often, and we end up with nothing in common. Then I'll demand change or file for divorce, but otherwise it is my solemn vow to stay together."

Let's take our vows seriously—God does.

A little side note. God does not want one of His daughters in harm's way, so if you are experiencing physical or mental abuse, seek help immediately. Taking action to move yourself to a safe place is critical and may be your first step to healing. Then wait upon the Lord for direction. You can still maintain your vow but do it from a place of safety while waiting for God's instruction.

When we pray to God for help, we are asking for God's will to be done. We should never desire anything but God's will. When we seek His will, we can't attach hidden clauses or provisions to what part of His Word we will obey. Don't pick and choose the verses you agree with and will follow and discard the ones that seem too hard to obey. That would be like deciding which signs on the road you will or won't obey while driving. If you decided to obey the speed limit but not the stop signs, eventually you would crash and cause damage—possibly serious injury or even death. The same thing can happen in our homes. If you want to avoid collisions in your marriage, obey the signs; otherwise the journey will be wrought with dangers and pitfalls that could have been easily avoided. If we disobey the rules and a head-on collision occurs, we are forced to look in the mirror to see who is at fault.

We can place our own minefields in our marriage when we tell God, "Lord, I want Your will in my marriage, but I cannot respect this man." Or with arms crossed, we state, "I will serve my husband, but God can't be serious about the submission thing. Come on—this isn't the '50s." There are no default clauses in God's word. The only fine print we should focus on is what is written in black, white, and red on the gold-leafed pages of our Bibles. God has given us a marriage recipe that truly has all the answers to life's journey, and His words will bring healing to even the most crippled marriage.

If we want to see changes in our relationship, instead of crying "Lord, fix him!" we should plead, "Lord, help me to be the best wife I can be." When we ask God to do a work in our own hearts—understanding that God is using our husbands, flawed and all, to teach *us* how to be more like Jesus—then the changes will start. Until we reach that point of clarity, we get in the way of God's perfect plan for our marriage. Remember, He called us to die to self. The "Me, Myself and I" bedsore is really what is irritating us. We point our finger to blame anyone but ourselves, wanting desperately for our husbands to change, when what God wants is change in *both* of us. The transformations in our husbands will often be a byproduct of our own modifications. God's ways are not our ways, His thoughts are not our thoughts.[36]

God is doing a work in His way and in His timing. Sometimes, God decides to use our husbands as the tool to sand off some of our own rough edges. Some of us require a small emery board to get rid of those bumpy patches, whereas some of us need a Sears power sander! Whatever the case, submit to God and allow Him to do the work. Don't pull the plug when things hurt a bit, or you'll cause a delay to the renovation God has in store. He wants you to take up your mat and be healed.

Rather than viewing marriage as an institution designed to bring you happiness, think of it as the boot camp God designed to help form you into a person more like Jesus. In the end, the finished product will be a masterpiece shaped by our Master Carpenter. Will you join me in deciding to take up your mat? Let's do this God's way and watch some miracles happen. In the next chapter, we'll look at some practical ways to obey God despite discouraging circumstances.

Challenge

What is one change I can make starting today to deepen my sensitivity and ministry to my husband? An area that perhaps God has been calling me to do that I have been putting off and, in essence, been disobedient? Perhaps it's respecting my husband with my words and actions or offering him grace and mercy, from one sinner to another. Write this change on a 3x5 card as a reminder to do that one thing and start today.

Six

Heaven's Kitchen

I've found the recipe for being happy whether full or hungry, hands full or hands empty. Whatever I have, wherever I am, I can make it through anything in the One who makes me who I am.

- Philippians 4:10 MSG

o you enjoy creating in the kitchen? My DNA doesn't seem to include the *love-to-cook* gene; however, I enjoy preparing foods that I know in advance will turn out delicious—one of those tried and true recipes that comes with the hopeful query, "Are there seconds?" When something is prepared correctly and has delicious flavor and aroma, my family wants to pull up their chairs, sit around the table and enjoy the food and the fellowship that comes with the tasty concoction. They've tasted the results and want more.

I've been told I make a fabulous Mud Pie.[37] I enjoy making this dessert for family and friends because everyone raves about how scrumptious it is—a heavenly, buttery Oreo cookie crust, mounds of mint chocolate chip and chocolate fudge ice cream layered with an incredible ooey-gooey fudge sauce, topped with whipped cream and chocolate shavings. Yum! My Mud Pie is not fantastic because I'm a fantastic cook. It's plate-licking good because I follow the directions of the skilled chef who went to culinary school and created the recipe. If I stray from her directions and use low-fat margarine instead of butter or cornflakes for the crust instead of Oreos, the final product is not going to be as yummy as the creator meant it to be. For guaranteed success, I need to use the ingredients and directions called out by the one who designed the recipe.

The same is true for our marriages. The Bible holds the formula for a delicious product and the One who created marriage wrote the recipe. Whether you are married to Prince Charming, or a Horny Toad, if you follow the directions the Master Chef has called us to follow, the product can turn out well. God will be there right alongside you to assist you, but it's up to you and me to put in the correct ingredients and follow the detailed instructions.

Like it or not, an enemy is warring against us hoping to wreak havoc on our ingredients list, but when we lean on the Creator, He will help us measure correctly and smooth out the lumps.

What if I opened the cookbook and tried to make Mud Pie merely by looking at the *picture* of the finished product instead of following the *recipe*? I could hazard a guess at the ingredients and directions based on the picture, but the end result would not be what the chef had in mind. The crust might be too hard to cut because I used too much butter, or the fudge sauce may be too thick to pour over the ice cream because it simmered too long.

> *The Bible holds the formula for a delicious product and the One who created marriage wrote the recipe.*

Sometimes we do this very thing with our marriages. We think we know what a good marriage looks like, so we hazard a guess at the ingredients and how to blend them together. But have we consulted the actual recipe?

God created the marriage relationship, and He has provided the directions for a successful and long-lasting marriage. We simply need to be willing to consult the recipe and then follow the step-by-step procedures to create a good product. If we are only willing to put in enough time to simply look at the pictures and arbitrarily follow what we think is the method, the results will be mediocre at best and a complete failure at worst.

Let's consider baking a simple cake—the kind you made in Cooking 101. However, we're not going to follow a recipe. We know the basic ingredients that go into a cake, so we'll wing it. I'm sure we can end up with an edible product. After all, we know how to make a cake, right?

First, let's dump all the ingredients that we *think* go into a cake into a large bowl. A scoop of flour, scoop of sugar, scoop of salt, scoop of baking soda—not really measuring, just scooping. Toss an egg in, blend everything together, just enough to get the ingredients moist, and then dump the lump of batter into pans that have not been prepared because we don't bother to take that step. Pop the pans into an oven that has not been preheated because that would have been step number one in the recipe we aren't following. Let's guess at the oven temperature—450°F should do since we need to get that oven hot as quickly as possible. We'll guess at the baking time, set the timer for an hour, and we're done.

Or so we thought. Ten minutes into the baking time, we remember that most cake recipes call for three eggs, and we only put in one. To make sure we have *all* the ingredients required for a great cake, we open the oven door, pull out the rack, crack open two eggs, and plop them on top of the cooking batter. Now all the components are in the pan, and we just need to wait for the batter to bake.

The initial cleanup is a breeze because we hadn't measured anything and only used one bowl. However, can you picture how our end product turned out? Probably something like this—a flat, burnt, crumbly, salty, crispy cake with two cooked eggs staring at us!

What a disaster—we definitely don't want to sink our teeth into this dessert! I could try to make the cake *look* nice on the outside by placing it on a fancy platter and smothering it with a tub of Betty Crocker frosting and candy sprinkles. But neither a fancy cake plate nor any amount of icing will turn this disaster into a decent cake. Inside it's literally junk food because the recipe was not consulted, ingredients were left out or measured incorrectly, and the cooking time and oven temperature were wrong. We might have thought we were "doing our best" and only cutting a few corners. But that is where the trouble lies in most marriages. We think cutting a few corners or leaving out a few ingredients won't make that much difference. We blend the recipes for marriage that we watched our parents live out and add in a few tips we learned from Dr. Phil and Oprah. Then we combine some examples we witnessed in the marriages of our friends or family with what we read in Cosmopolitan, and we think if we dump it all into our marriage, it will "all just turn out" in the end.

Be careful this does not happen in your marriage. If we don't take the time and effort to check God's recipe and follow His directions, we will end up with a hot mess—flat, brittle, and unsavory. If we "wing it" and guess at God's instructions, we might have some of the right ingredients in the mix. But most recipes will not turn out if we add too much of one item or too little of another. If the ingredients are not blended the right way, we'll have salty and bitter bites throughout, and we'll be tempted to throw the whole thing in the dumpster.

We need to consult the Master Chef. If we slip into the habit of guessing at the ingredients and skipping important directions, we run the risk of wasted efforts and a house full of strife. We can be prone to leaving out the tablespoon of respect and substituting with heaping cups of nagging and PMS. If we want our marriages to turn out right and be the kind of relationship that people want to sit around the table and enjoy, we need to decide to give God's recipe a try.

Let's bake a second cake. This time we check the ingredients and follow the directions, consulting the recipe in a way that would make our Home Economics teacher proud. Measuring everything takes a little longer and using the best ingredients might be more expensive, but a beautiful end product is worth the extra time and expenditure.

If the recipe calls for one teaspoon of salt, don't use a tablespoon or question if you really need the salt at all. The creator found that a little bit of salt would enhance the flavor, but too much would make the cake overly salty. Keep in mind that each ingredient on its own might not taste good at all. Imagine eating a teaspoonful of baking soda or drinking a cup of egg white—yuck! Similarly, submission on its own might seem too hard to swallow, but when blended with the other ingredients, it's an important part of creating a quality product. If we decide to leave respect out of our marriages or use only a pinch instead of the teaspoon that is required, we will end up with a flat marriage. Each ingredient is important, but some are critical.

In my first marriage, I was prone to leaving out the crucial ingredient of respect. I allowed my husband's actions and behaviors to dictate whether or not that measurement of respect would be blended in, sprinkled in as an afterthought, or left out altogether. When we choose to leave respect out of our marriages, we are cutting off our noses to spite our faces. Or as Proverbs 14:1 (AMP) puts it:

> But the foolish woman [who lacks spiritual insight] tears
> [her house] down with her own hands [by ignoring godly principles].
> Proverbs 14:1 AMP

Strong words from God's cookbook. Because respect is such an important component, we discuss practical ways to implement respect in an upcoming chapter.

Our method is equally as important as our ingredients. If the recipe says to sift, then sift if you want the best cake you can make. The result of skipping that step might not be immediately apparent, just like disrespecting our husbands here and there might not create havoc in our marriages right away. But, it will affect the quality of the end product. Each and every step God transcribes is there for a reason—He does not waste words.

The stars in the sky and the earth beneath your feet will pass away

before one letter of God's rules for living become worthless.

- Luke 16:17 VOICE

Back in the day, before the wonderful invention of the Mix Master, most cake recipes called for "blending the batter for 200 strokes." This was the best way to get the lumps out; however, this becomes tedious when you get to 66...67...68. We find ourselves doing many monotonous tasks as wives, don't we? Picking his wet towel off the floor for the 66th time, cleaning his socks and underwear for the 67th time, making the bed by yourself for the 68th time. And don't get me started on how many ways we can cook a chicken! Monotony.

> *The key to moving from a dreary, tedious perspective to cheerful, alive contentment is to change our attitude and outlook.*

When the sink seems to fill itself with dirty dishes, the laundry basket constantly overflows, and you don't have the energy to run one more errand, stop and pray. Stop Satan from stealing your joy. Remind yourself to give thanks and press on. Be thankful for the food that makes the dishes dirty, for the clothes that fill the basket, and for the chicken you get to cook. Focus on things that are lovely and true[38]—your joy will conquer the monotonous. It's all about having the right attitude.

The key to moving from a dreary, tedious perspective to cheerful, alive contentment is to change our attitude and outlook. What if we changed our perspective? Our Master Chef tells us in His recipe book to work willingly at whatever you do, as though you were working for the Lord rather than for men.[39] Remember that the Lord will give you an inheritance as your reward, and the

Master you are serving is Christ.[40]

In other words, do the laundry as unto the Lord. Make the bed as unto the Lord. Cook that chicken as unto the Lord. This attitude shift will make all the difference in the world. The enemy wants us to resent our husbands and our household chores, so he can lure us to a place of discontentment. However, if we simply change our viewpoint and focus on the blessing of having a bed to make, clothes that need cleaning, and even a husband to do life with, then a smile can replace the pouty two-year-old defiant scowl that sometimes shows up. Be thankful we *have* a husband to do laundry for when many go to bed alone each night. Satan wants us to moan about what we don't have instead of choosing to focus on what we do have. It's how he worked in the very beginning when he whispered to Eve, "Did God really say you must not eat the fruit from any of the trees in the garden?"[41] Satan lured Eve into feeling discontent—let's not join her in biting into that apple.

I know this can be difficult, especially when your heart might be so cold towards your husband because of things he does or doesn't do—joy has ebbed away. I struggled with this too for many years. I constantly ran to my Heavenly Father and begged Him to change my heart and to give me the desire to obey His Word and the ability to love and respect my husband. God is always faithful—keep going to Him for strength. He always provides. We simply need to be willing to go to Him, listen and obey—and respect His timing.

It is so worth it in the long run to take the extra time to follow God's recipe—use the correct ingredients and don't take shortcuts. Our marriages will be sweeter and more palatable; there will be fewer lumps and less of a mess to clean up. Obedience will be rewarded with blessings.

What exactly does God's recipe say about marriage, and is this a recipe

I can actually follow? Some people just don't have the skills to make a Baked Alaska, even if they follow the directions. The good news is God doesn't ask us to do things He won't empower us to do. With God in your kitchen, you can even follow a Baked Alaska recipe and have a fabulous end result—just take it one step and one ingredient at a time. When the recipe says to whip up that meringue and broil it to tinged brown perfection, God will be by your side to help you with every step.

When we prepared the failed cake, we didn't bother to prep the pans, so this time around we will grease them so the cake will pop out easily. Preheat that oven to the infamous 350°F so the cake will heat evenly and cook properly. Set the timer for thirty-five minutes and take the cake out when we hear the buzzer ring. Wait for the cake to cool *before* smoothing on the icing. Producing an end product you can be proud of takes preparation, timing, and waiting, but there is always a purpose to the Master Chef's ingredients and directions.

Compare our two end products. What a contrast! The cake that took more time and effort is markedly more beautiful to the eye and more delicious to the taste buds.

One cake is dry, salty, crusty, and unappetizing. The other is moist, sweet, delicious and presentable—you want more. The first cake was the product of winging it, merely guessing at ingredients and methods, and taking shortcuts. The other was born out of consulting, checking, and adhering to the instructions. Which end product do you want to serve in your home? A wise woman will choose to follow the Master Chef's plan and consequently enjoy the delicious chocolate cake. A foolish woman will wing it when it comes to things of great importance.

Admittedly, not following the directions was faster and easier. Guessing and simply dumping ingredients into a bowl was amusing. The same holds true for our marriages—not following the directions is certainly easier and can be more fun—in the beginning. The book of Hebrews reminds us that sin does offer fleeting pleasures.[42]

Having a ladies' night out every night and not bothering to cook or clean for our husband and family would be simpler and seemingly carefree. We could go to dinner with a friend Monday night, play Bunco on Tuesday, attend an essential oils party on Wednesday, Bible study on Thursday, then round off the week with a chick flick on Friday. Just leave a note on the kitchen table that reads, "Be back later. Dinner's in the freezer."

Why bother cleaning the house? It will just get messy again tomorrow, and no one else ever helps anyway. Why plan meals for the family every week when our guys can pick up Taco Bell on their way home from work? Why take the time to make ourselves look nice for our husbands? We're already married. Plus, he let himself go, too. Why can't I make jokes or tell stories at my husband's expense to get a laugh? It's all just innocent fun, right?

If we employ any of these attitudes, we will eventually end up with a failed marriage—the brittle, flat, crumbly type that is bitter when you bite into it. Don't enjoy the fleeting pleasures of sin as sin leads to death[43]—possibly even the death of your marriage.

Determine today that you want a Chocolate Cake Marriage. Decide to follow God's recipe. The joy and peace will be so worth it in the end. Just keep that picture of the perfectly-baked chocolate cake close by and remember that is the goal as you start to follow the recipe one step at a time.

Challenge

Make a Blessing Flip Calendar. Get thirty-one 3x5 index cards and punch two holes in the top of each. Jot down on each card one thing that you love, appreciate, or respect about your husband. For example, he puts gas in the car, brings you flowers, helps with the dishes, goes faithfully to his job each day, etc. Tie a ribbon through the holes and number each card 1 through 31. We now have a flip calendar to remind us why we fell in love with our husbands in the first place.

This little stack of reminders can be a surprisingly useful tool for several reasons. First of all, as we make our lists, we will be reminded of the things our husbands do that we appreciate. As women, we tend to have an elephant memory for how our husbands irritate or annoy us, but we let their good qualities slip into the "can't access that file" part of our memory. If it's difficult to think of thirty-one actions, reflect back to when you were dating or during your early years of marriage. We can remember things we love and appreciate if we try—we married these guys so we really liked them a lot at one point!

Our new calendar will also be a good reminder of our husband's positive qualities during those spells when he is on our last nerve—let these cards be a memory jogger for why we said, "I do." Hopefully, our personalized Blessing Flip Calendar will warm our heart and help us to keep no record of wrongs, only a record of rights.

> *[Love] does not dishonor others, it is not self-seeking, it is not easily*
> *angered, it keeps no record of wrongs.*
> - 1 Corinthians 13:5 NIV

Great benefits can come from our husbands seeing the compiled list. They might not be aware of what they do that bless us. We just might find they'll do some of these more often now that they know of our gratitude.

Seven

What's in Your Cake?

Yeast, too, is a "small thing," but it works its way through a whole batch of bread dough pretty fast. So get rid of this "yeast." Our true identity is flat and plain, not puffed up with the wrong kind of ingredient.

- 1 Corinthians 5:6b-7 MSG

One of the first things a chef does when baking a cake is to check the ingredients list for the recipe. She needs to know what she has to purchase and what she already has in her pantry. Our marriage ingredients should include love, joy, peace, patience, kindness, goodness, faithfulness, gentleness, and self-control.[44]

Since love is one of the most important ingredients, we need to know our husband's love language. Gary Chapman's book *The Five Love Languages* is an excellent tool to increase your awareness of what makes your husband feel loved. Take the online test at www.5lovelanguages.com for a fun and easy way to become bi-lingual.

What if I called out to my husband every morning, "Nakupenda! Nakupenda! Nakupenda!"? Would he be blessed by that? Would he understand what I was expressing? If he gave me a puzzled look, but I just kept repeating it, he'd probably get irritated with me. However, if I said "Nakupenda" to a group in South Africa, they would probably smile and maybe even give me a hug. In Swahili, Nakupenda means, "I love you." Since my husband doesn't speak Swahili, he would have no idea that I was trying to communicate "I love you." If we don't know our husband's love language, they may feel unloved and frustrated despite our effort to express our love to them. Don't waste "Nakupenda" on your spouse today—speak love in a way he understands.

If your husband's love language is one-on-one time and he likes basketball, watch an occasional game with him. Cuddle up next to him even if you have 100 other things on your to-do list. Once in a while, you can set some of those tasks aside and spend time with your man—he needs you to. Our husbands want our companionship, particularly when quality time is their love language.

Words of affirmation are another way to speak love to your spouse. Encourage your husband each day with uplifting words that speak confidence and respect. If this is his language, he will hear you speaking love.

Physical touch can speak volumes as well. If this is your man's dialect, get physical! Even if that is not your love language, you need to make the effort in obedience to God's word because He gifted your body to your husband. Let him unwrap it.

Speaking of gifts, that is another way to show love to your man. Buy him his favorite snack when you are at the grocery store or pick him up something special when you are at the mall or shopping online. Do special things even when it's not his birthday or Valentine's Day—your thoughtfulness will speak volumes.

If we were sitting together as friends over a cup of coffee or tea, I would take this moment to get serious with you. To look you in the eyes, in love, and say, "We need to get serious about protecting our marriages." There is a woman out there who will make time for your husband. She will tell him that he's sexy and handsome. She will buy him gifts, write him love notes, and show him respect. She will even unwrap her body and present it to your husband. Look at the warnings God Himself shares with us.

> *It was at twilight, in the evening, as deep darkness fell. The woman approached him, seductively dressed and sly of heart. She was the brash, rebellious type, never content to stay at home. She is often in the streets and markets, soliciting at every corner. She threw her arms around him and kissed him, and with a brazen look she said, "I've just made my peace offerings and fulfilled my vows. You're the one I was looking for! I came out to find you, and here you are! My bed is spread with beautiful blankets, with colored sheets of Egyptian linen. I've perfumed my bed with myrrh, aloes, and cinnamon. Come, let's drink our fill of love until morning. Let's enjoy each other's caresses for my husband is not home. He's away on a long trip. He has taken a wallet full of money with him and won't return until later this month."*
>
> *- Proverbs 7:9-20*

She seduced him with her pretty speech and enticed him with her flattery. This type of woman drove through my neighborhood a couple of years ago. I know it was her because the license plate frame on her blue convertible read, "My other ride is your husband." This woman took the time to find a screwdriver, twist the screws, and put that frame on her

We need to get serious about protecting our marriages.

vehicle to boldly proclaim that our husbands are her prey.

I encountered this type of woman in my first marriage when my husband and I were attending a wedding. She complimented me on my dress as we sat in the church pew witnessing the bride and groom exchange their vows, and then she seduced my husband hours later at the reception. Beware. We are warned in God's recipe book to be alert to the enemy's schemes.

> *Stay alert! Watch out for your great enemy, the devil.*
> *He prowls around like a roaring lion, looking for someone to devour.*
> *Stand firm against him and be strong in your faith.*
> *- 1 Peter 5:8-9a*

The Message translation puts it this way:

> *Keep a cool head. Stay alert. The Devil is poised to pounce, and would like nothing better than to catch you napping. Keep your guard up.*

During the reception, when I saw my husband go outside to smoke, I chose to stay seated alone at our table. I was not alert, not standing firm, not realizing that the enemy was prowling, looking to devour our marriage. I was not praying that my husband would stay faithful. I was not asking God, "Should I go outside with him?" Instead, with my own private pity party underway, I nursed the hurt feelings that he had left me seated alone...again.

The woman God speaks about in Proverbs 7 is on the prowl today. She is alive and well. Choose to stand firm against the enemy, and ask God to lead and guide your *every* step. I let my bitterness towards my husband pull my guard down and open the door for the seduction. I'm not suggesting that this placed all the blame on my shoulders. Our husbands are called to be faithful and protective. I should not have been left alone for over an hour at a dinner table. However, we need to be on guard and aware of the prowling lion.

Our marriages are targets in the enemy's shooting gallery. Don't be fooled into a mindset that you can put your relationship with your husband on cruise control and hope you reach the destination of wedded bliss. We need to guard our marriages vigilantly and do all we can to protect them against the tricks and schemes of Satan. I have journeyed through the dark valley of divorce and would not wish that trek on my worst enemy. God has reason to hate divorce—it leaves scars on more than two people.

To stand firm and place a strong fortress around our relationships involves another key ingredient that must be poured into and over our marriages—heaping cupfuls of prayer. Most cake recipes include instructions to "prepare the pans." For this step, I typically grab my trusty can of Pam™. A couple of healthy sprays onto metal bakeware, and the cakes will pop right out. An invisible coating that no one else sees makes all the difference when the time comes to pop the cakes out on to the pretty platter. Without it, things can get messy. With it, the cakes come out with ease. This behind-the-scenes spritz represents prayer for our husband. No one sees we are praying for him just like no one sees the spritz of Pam, but prayer will make all the difference in the ease of our relationship with our man. God tells us over and over in His Word about the importance of prayer. Even Jesus knew the importance of seeking His Father's face.

But Jesus often withdrew to lonely places and prayed.

- Luke 5:16 NIV

Ask yourself this question: If you are not praying for your husband, then who is? Ponder that for a moment. Maybe he has a godly mother and father who lift him up in prayer, but if not, who is going to our Heavenly Father on behalf of our man, pleading for protection, faithfulness, health, integrity, and safety? Praying that he will be a good provider, a caring husband, and a discerning father? The enemy is after our men, sweet sister, and he is luring, deceiving, and tempting as only the devil can. He is a formidable foe, but God is infinitely more powerful and calls us to put on the armor of God and pray constantly.[45]

Let's ask God to put a hedge of protection around our husband. Request that our omnipotent, omnipresent, and omniscient Mighty God keeps our husband faithful and helps him to be a better husband and father. Plead with our Abba Father for our husband to have favor at his workplace, integrity in all his dealings, loyalty to us and our family, dependability as a friend, the heart of a servant, and a desire to love his enemies. And, most importantly, implore our Father in heaven to give our man a hunger for God's Word and a desire to glorify God in everything he thinks, says, and does.

We must take the enemy's threats seriously and combat them with the shield of faith, protected by the helmet of salvation and the sword of the Spirit.[46] Perhaps you can take a couple of minutes right now to pray for your husband. Pray too that God will mature you to be the best wife you can be. I often pray that God will keep my heart pliable to hear what He wants me to hear and then to give me the courage and strength to take action on what He calls me to do. We need all the help we can get, amen?

We are directed to love and honor our husbands every day—not just on the days he helps with the dishes and remembers to take out the trash. Every day also means the days when all he seems to care about is ESPN or his phone, he forgets to bring flowers home for a special occasion, or he has grown horns because PMS has reared its ugly head.

Proverbs 31:12 (NIV) says, *"She brings him good, not harm, all the days of her life."*

We don't need to check Webster's Dictionary to learn what *all* means. *All* means *all*—the whole, entire, total amount. Bringing him good every day is a tall order, but again, God does not ask us to do what He won't give us the power to do. If we desire to do everything as unto the Lord, He will help us. We simply have to decide if we want the flat, brittle egg sandwich cake or the sweet, moist, chocolate cake.

Once that is decided, where do we begin? How do we get out of the funk we're in? What if we're not in love anymore? What if our holy matrimony looks more like unruly roommates? Are we supposed to tolerate certain behaviors that are wrong? We know we're not supposed to nag, but what if he never listens? Some days are easier than others, but what do we do when following the recipe is too hard? I want the *How to Have a Joyous Marriage in 10 Easy Steps* handbook.

We need to decide to make the changes God wants us to make—one moment at a time, one day at a time—altering our behaviors and attitudes. We don't make a cake with the snap of our fingers. We fashion it one step at a time. As we follow the directions, we see the cake come together. Our marriage can slowly come together too—start with one ingredient at a time. Be patient with yourself. Our marriages are a work in progress, and we are a work in progress—God *will* complete the work He has begun,[47] but there is time between the start and the finish.

The recipe we are following is found on the pages of the best-selling book of all time. The Author of this incredible manual created you and your husband and even allowed the union of the two of you. Even if you think you are a mismatched couple, God says *you are no longer two, but one.*[48]

Considering the Author made both of you, and designed the covenant of marriage, why would we look to anyone but Him for answers and guidance? We don't need to run to the nearest counseling center and pay $80 an hour if our marriage is flat and brittle. Check the recipe again, and we might find we left out one or two ingredients or skipped a couple of steps. God wants to get us back on track, and He is always there to lead and guide. There is nothing wrong with seeking counsel, just make sure our Wonderful Counselor has been consulted and heeded first. You just might save a gob of money.

> *... And he will be called Wonderful Counselor, Mighty God,*
> *Everlasting Father, Prince of Peace.*
> - Isaiah 9:6b NIV

Change takes change. If we want lasting transformation in our marriage, we need to be willing to take the time and make the effort to follow the recipe. Without change, the things we do will remain the things we do.

Name a person on the planet who wants a stagnant, bitter marriage. No one, right? Yet so few are willing to stir out the lumps that cause the bitterness. If we don't work at our marriages, it won't be long before the romantic memories of the honeymoon fade away. We might find ourselves smack dab in the middle of a freshly dug rut—and we are often the one found holding the shovel. There is an old saying: "A grave is nothing more than a rut with the ends capped off." Get out of the rut before it becomes a grave with the tombstone of your marriage on top. God would hate that.

"For I hate divorce!" says the LORD.

-Malachi 2:16a

Therefore, what God has united and joined together,

man must not separate [by divorce].

- Mark 10:9 AMP

If you look up the word "rut" in your trusty thesaurus, you'll find depression as one of its synonyms. Interesting. If a cloud of gloom hangs over your marriage, instead of reaching for the Prozac, step out from beneath those cumulus clouds and get back on God's path for your marriage. He declares:

He provides me rest in rich, green fields beside streams

of refreshing water. He soothes my fears;

- Psalm 23:2 VOICE

Are you willing to follow? He won't force you to, but His path is always the best one.

He will not lead us down a dead-end path. If you find yourself feeling you are at an impasse, you were fooled into following the wrong leader. Remember, the enemy is on the prowl and looking for ways to deceive us. God can show us how to make the U-turn to get back on the right track. We can start making changes today by spinning around, rechecking the recipe, and allowing God to lead us. It's *never* too late. Remember, with God *all* things are possible.[49]

Again, God likes to use the word *all*. He doesn't say "*some* things are possible" or "*most* things are possible." Yes, God says, "*ALL* things are possible." Even if the things in our world *seem* hopeless or feel impossible today, God is still the Hope-giver! He can make all things new, but we need to be willing to obey Him and follow His directions. Let's determine right now to follow His lead.

God is called our Good Shepherd, and a shepherd leads and protects his sheep. God is not our Good *Herder*, or Good *Wrangler*, but our Good *Shepherd*. The analogy is not lost when you know about sheep. They can be somewhat stupid at times, prone to wander and quite vulnerable. Don't be offended by that—it's just straight-up truth. Like humans, sheep need a shepherd to guide them to the best place for their safety, health and tranquility. Without someone to lead and guide them, sheep will walk in the same rut for days, weeks, and even months. Malnourishment and weakness become their companions without a shepherd because their food source depletes, predators move in, and fear overtakes them. Nothing is left to eat alongside their rut but wood, hay and stubble. A good shepherd continuously leads his flock to green pastures for healthy nourishment and away from danger to protect his flock from predators and unsafe conditions. A Good Shepherd can be the difference between life and death.

For years, I cried desperately to God for help in my first marriage as we were in a well-traveled rut. Discouragement and despondency ran deep. The voice of my Shepherd called me to respect and submit to my husband; however, my hardened heart crossed its arms and refused to obey everything God instructed me to do. I needed someone to remind me that praying for God to show me what to do in a crisis often involves *doing.* When the engine light beams from the dashboard of our car, it reminds us to add oil. Knowing we *need* oil will not lube the engine. Actually pouring oil in solves the issue. We need to be willing to act on what God tells us to do if we want healing in our marriages—especially if we just don't feel like it.

God wants *us* to change *us*, not our husbands. Grasp this concept, and we will have a far greater chance of transformation in our marriages. God did not appoint us to be our husband's Holy Spirit. Our heavenly Father wants us to become more like His Son, Jesus, and to glorify our Father in heaven.

God *will* work on our husband. Yes, changes need to be made in him, too. We are all supposed to be growing and maturing. Aren't you glad you are not the same person you were in high school? The important thing for you and me is to be willing to sense the changes the Lord wants us to make. Our heavenly Father will do a mighty work in our husbands if we will step aside. Get out of God's way. Release our husband to the Lord and let Him do His stuff. At the same time, decide to be a doer of God's Word in our own thoughts and actions. Become a woman after God's heart.

Take a moment to stop and pray right now. Ask the Lord to give you the desire to love your husband unconditionally—and to lean into the changes that He is calling you to make.

"Father in Heaven, You are so worthy of praise. I acknowledge that without You, I can do nothing. You will be my guide even to the end. You have a perfect plan for my life, Lord. Lead me and guide me in Your truths. Show me how to be more like You—unendingly patient and forgiving. Holy Spirit, refine me, remove my imperfections. I want to be the wife You desire me to be. Help me to get my eyes off my needs and on to the needs of my mate. Please show me the areas I need to change, and empower me to make the necessary improvements. I want to be obedient to You—not just a woman who knows Your Word, but one who obeys it.   In Jesus Name, I pray. Amen."

Then you can tell the next generation detail by detail the story of God, Our God forever, who guides us till the end of time.

- Psalm 48:13b-14 MSG

Challenge

Ask yourself, "Who have I been listening to when checking the ingredients in my marriage? Is the counsel improving the product, or are the instructions leaving me with the same brittle, flat marriage? Does what 'they'" suggest line up with what the Bible instructs?"

Determine today to seek God's counsel first. God will show you how to blend the ingredients, and He promises to draw near to you as you draw near to Him. A bite of chocolate cake sounds really good!

God's blessings follow you and await you at every turn: when you don't follow the advice of those who delight in wicked schemes, When you avoid sin's highway, when judgment and sarcasm beckon you, but you refuse.

Psalm 1:1 VOICE

Eight

The Secret Ingredient

Only the Eternal knows the secret things. But we and our
descendants are always responsible for what has been
revealed to us, and we need to obey every word of this law.

Deuteronomy 29:29 VOICE

What is a BLT sandwich without the bacon? A cheeseburger without the cheese? Chocolate cake without the chocolate? Would anyone decide to leave out these critical ingredients—on purpose?

Some ingredients are so vital that the product will not pass the muster without it. As we discussed earlier, when it comes to a Chocolate Cake Marriage, the crucial ingredient—the one you just can't leave out—is respect. Our husbands need, crave, live for, must have, and will die without respect. Leaving respect out of your marriage is parallel to leaving chocolate out of your chocolate cake—you won't enjoy a slice without it. Add respect, and you'll see palpable changes.

Do you remember this scene from the movie *Notting Hill*? Julia Roberts' character, Anna Scott, a famous movie star, falls in love with William Thacker, a used bookstore owner played by Hugh Grant. Their roller coaster romance provides lots of laughs and drama in this fun romantic comedy. During one scene, Anna says to William, "I'm just a girl, standing in front of a boy, asking him to love me."

> *Respect is the key ingredient for any relationship we have with males in our lives.*

As women, we can relate to this statement and maybe even shed a tear at the endearing vulnerability. We understand Anna's desire to be loved because women tend to crave love. Our husbands, on the other hand, have a completely different need. Men crave respect. If our movie plot were reversed, William would say to Anna, "I'm just a boy standing in front of a girl asking her to respect me."

Respect is the key ingredient for any relationship we have with males in our lives—son, father, brother, co-worker, but especially with our husband.

Our husbands literally *need* respect; they don't just *want it*. Respect is oxygen to their souls. As women, we might not understand this because we need love. Yes, we want to be respected, but we don't *need* it in comparison to our male counterparts.

Men and women are so very different. In his book, *Love and Respect*, Dr. Emerson Eggerich describes it this way: "...women look at and hear the world through pink sunglasses and pink hearing aids, while men look at and hear the world through blue sunglasses and blue hearing aids.[50]"

God created men and women to receive and process life differently. Instead of fighting these differences, we can choose to embrace them and respect our husbands for how God made them. Adding respect could be all your marriage needs for a miraculous change—similar to waving a magic wand.

We talked earlier about love languages—discovering the best way to communicate love to our husband based on his particular love language—whether to spend one-on-one time with him, or to pour out words of affirmation in order to fill his love tank. However, love language is not as important as respect language. We must all speak respect to our husbands or our marriages *will* falter or fail completely. If we are not fluent in respect and this language is not woven into every sentence we speak, we might as well press the mute button on the other love languages. Your husband won't hear love when disrespect drowns out every other word.

You can spend all the one-on-one time you are able to with your man, cook him his favorite meal every night, and even show up naked in the bedroom once in a while. But if you are not respecting him, instead of the sweet chocolate morsels you were hoping for, you will inevitably end up with the flat, brittle, burnt cake instead.

God's word is very direct.

> *However, each one of you also must love his wife as he loves himself, and the wife must respect her husband.*
> - Ephesians 5:33 NIV

Perhaps this is a tall order because you might find it nearly impossible to truly respect your husband because of past hurts or present activities he's involved in. Remember, God will never ask us to do something that He will not enable and empower us to do. Ask Jesus to be your strength and to empower you to be obedient to His word. Several verses before Ephesians 5:33, God tells us:

> *Submit to one another out of reverence for Christ.*
> - Ephesians 5:21 NIV

Jesus calls us to submit to one another. Husbands love your wives, wives respect your husbands. It all comes down to deciding whether or not we are willing to obey the Lord and leave the results to the One who created marriage—the One who wants you to enjoy a Chocolate Cake Marriage.

If we will decide to truly become doers of the word, we could transform our marriages in a matter of days. The first time I read Ephesians 5:33, during my first marriage, I thought, "Yikes! How am I going to truly show respect to this man? So much of who he is I do not respect." I had allowed his use of marijuana and his disrespect for Christ to erode my respect for him. I could not comprehend how a father could use drugs while raising young sons. Even though I had smoked pot in my teens and early twenties, after I asked Christ into my life, Jesus took away the desire to get high. As I grew as a Christian, and slowly learned through scriptures and godly counsel, I came to understand that I could disagree with what the boys' father was doing yet still treat him with respect. In fact, God wanted me to do that. It's not always easy to respect our spouses, but God will provide the strength and power to obey ... and the blessings that comes from obedience will follow.

God does not call us to condone sin—ever. But He does call us to respect our husbands. I could have an attitude of respect yet still refuse to tolerate drug use in our home. Look at it this way—there are Commanders-in-Chief who we would rather not see in the White House because of the activities and agendas they promote. However, as Ambassadors for Christ, I hope we would treat any president with respect by modeling courteous and reverent behavior in their presence. This same concept holds true in our relationship with our husbands. Even if there are activities he takes part in that we disagree with, we can still model an attitude of respect and reverence. Leave the convicting of the sin to the Holy Spirit.

Emerson Eggerichs describes it this way in his book, *Love and Respect*:

"Ultimately, you practice love or respect because beyond your spouse you see Jesus Christ and you envision a moment when you will be standing before Him at the final judgment, realizing that your marriage was really a tool and a test to deepen and demonstrate your love and your reverence for your Lord."

We should respect and submit to our husbands as unto the Lord.

Have you ever felt your husband's activities or agendas are strangling the love and respect you want to have for him? God tells us if we will humble ourselves, seek His face and obey His word, He will heal us.[51] Just say *yes* to obedience and watch God work miracles. Again, He will not call us to do something He cannot empower us to do. The question is: Are we willing to seek His face and obey His word?

Our husbands need us to pour heaping spoonfuls of respect into our marriages to create that triple-layered chocolate cake covered in chocolate shavings. Men need respect like we need chocolate, or our morning cup of java, or even love. It can be difficult for women to completely understand how essential respect is because as women, we need love far more than we need respect. And, it is typically easier for us to demonstrate love than it is to model respect.

Not that we don't want to be respected, but love really makes us tick. The opposite is true for most men. Love is nice, but respect is vital—without it, they will become withdrawn and quick-tempered. As wives, we are often not even aware of our disrespectful actions. On a number of occasions, my husband has shared with me that I had shown him a lack of respect, and yet I did not even realize that my actions or words had come across disrespectfully. It is crucial for us to learn what feels disrespectful to our men or we might unintentionally pour a cupful of disrespect into our batter.

Respect is defined as a feeling or understanding that someone or something is important and should be treated in an appropriate way.[52]

That means, God wants us to treat our husbands in an appropriate way as someone who is important. It sounds so elementary, yet as we dig a little deeper we might find we are disrespecting our husbands without even realizing it.

Some light is shed on what respect looks like when we read 1 Peter 3:1-5:

> In the same way, you wives must accept the authority of your husbands. Then, even if some refuse to obey the Good News, your godly lives will speak to them without any words. They will be won over by observing your pure and reverent lives. Don't be concerned about the outward beauty of fancy hairstyles, expensive jewelry, or beautiful clothes. You should clothe yourselves instead with the beauty that comes from within, the unfading beauty of a gentle and quiet spirit, which is so precious to God. This is how the holy women of old made themselves beautiful. They put their trust in God and accepted the authority of their husbands.
>
> 1 Peter 3:1-5

Even if we are having a bad day or our husband is on our last nerve, we are called to respect and submit to him. God does not expect us to condone sin nor to be a doormat but to demonstrate respect and submission. Perhaps this will require leaning on God for the strength, power, and will to model respect, particularly if you are in a struggling marriage. Keep in mind, we want to create the sweet Chocolate Cake Marriage, so stay focused on the end result and follow the directions no matter how difficult the process might seem. Respect is that secret ingredient that will make all the difference—God is never wrong with His instructions.

Submission is not the "S-word" in marriage. Submitting *as unto the Lord* is the key. We are not called to submit to activities or requests that are sinful or abusive. For example, if your husband asks you to watch pornography with him as a little pre-love warm-up, the answer is no. If he asks you to sign a fraudulent tax form to save money, the answer is no. You are not to accept physical or verbal abuse under the banner of submission. If this is happening to you or someone you know, please seek help right away. Too many women live in fear because they believe they need to be submissive "no matter what." Perhaps God is calling them to take a stand. I lived under that thought for a long time in my first marriage—too afraid to take a stand instead of trusting God and "fearing not." Ask the Lord to show you and seek outside counsel if you need to.

Submitting as unto the Lord is key

I am cautious to say, though, that sometimes abuse occurs when a man has been disrespected so many times that he reaches a breaking point. This is absolutely not an excuse, and you should still seek immediate safety if abuse is occurring. On the same note, only you know if you are contributing in any way to hostilities and difficulties in your marriage by modeling disrespect. Inciting our husbands to wrath with a constant drip of disrespect can happen gradually and is one of the tools the enemy uses to bring discord and dissension. Be aware that disrespecting your husband is a surefire way of tearing down your own home.

> *A wise woman strengthens her family, but a foolish*
>
> *woman destroys hers by what she does.*
>
> - Proverbs 14:1 NCV

So, with that clarification in place, let's look at disrespectful behavior from a man's perspective, and then we will get practical. I know from my own marriage and after talking to thousands of women and quite a few men, we often times don't even realize we are disrespecting our husbands.

To give the essence of what I'm talking about, here is an anecdote from a male perspective written by Daniel Robertson, a Christian writer:[53]

THE SHOPPING INCIDENT EARLY IN OUR MARRIAGE

One day my wife and I went shopping at Costco. I began to lead her in one direction fully expecting her to come along with me, but instead she seemed upset and asked me where I was going. Being the boneheaded man that I am, I didn't tell her, but instead just motioned for her to follow me. Now she was beyond upset. In fact, she actually stormed off in the other direction. We did most of our shopping separately that day.

I was floored. I went to grab the double loaf of bread I had been aiming for, wondering what on Earth I had done wrong. I remember feeling very frustrated. Why couldn't she just follow my lead, I thought. Did I really need to explain to her that I just wanted to grab some bread?

Apparently, I made one other fatal mistake as well. The bread was at the front of the store. You never start at the front of the store. You go all the way to the back and work your way forward.

The point of the story is that I felt completely disrespected. All I wanted was for my wife to follow my lead through the store and not question which direction I was taking her.

Now, you might be thinking, what is *his* problem? Why couldn't he just love his wife as Christ loves the church and follow where she wanted to go? Remember, we are attempting to make changes in ourselves and letting God, our Creator, work on our guys. God truly is at work in them. Our job is not to point our finger at our husbands. Instead, let's peek in the mirror and find out where *we* need to make changes and let the Lord work on our husbands. I know there are many areas we may want to see changed, but in this book we are focusing on what we as wives can do to have a Chocolate Cake Marriage.

Obviously, the Robertsons were having communication issues. But we can endeavor to honor and respect our husbands in our daily activities—and have fun at the same time. When my husband and I go to Costco, I have that story in mind so I look forward to following him. And there are times when he blazes a trail in the opposite direction than I would go during solo Costco runs. But if I let the enemy have his way by demanding my own, I am tearing a brick from my own house—which will eventually leave it in rubbles. Instead, I hold my husband's hand, smile, and enjoy the samples along the way.

We can choose to respect and submit to our husbands as unto the Lord, and guess what will happen? God will bless us! Reflecting on the Robertsons' story, if Jesus Himself wanted you to follow Him at Costco, would you roll your eyes and stomp off to the back of the store instead? I hope your answer is, "No." Knowing Jesus wants the very best for us should cause us to want to follow Him and obey Him. Jesus is the one who tells us to submit to our husbands as unto the Lord—not our husbands.

When we follow Jesus, sometimes our road will have bumps and debris along the way. But if we are following Him, we can be assured we are on the right road going in the right direction. His way leads to abundant life. When God tells us to submit to our husbands *as unto the Lord*, He is saying: *Follow him as you would Jesus.* Are we willing to obey God? Are we ready to implement respect in our marriage? God wired our men to thrive on respect and without it, they can't be fully confident in their relationship with their wives.

> *Jesus is the one who tells us to submit to our husbands as unto the Lord*

When our husbands feels respected, they will be strong and confident in their marriage—and this will spill over into so many other aspects of who they are as men. But something as simple as not following his lead at the grocery store can start you down the path of what Dr. Eggerichs calls the "crazy cycle." If we leave respect out of our relationship, our husband may start to leave out love. This is comparable to purposely leaving the baking soda out of your cake batter. Perhaps it doesn't seem like it will make a huge difference—it's only a small amount of one simple ingredient. However, when you bite into what you were hoping to be sweet and delicious, and instead it's crusty and dry, we know where the mistake was made.

... and the wife must respect her husband.

- Ephesians 5:33b NIV

Only you and your husband can determine whether disrespect has found a home inside your four walls. Like termites, a lot of damage can be done before you even realize damage is occurring, so take action before the walls crumble.

If your marriage is in a rut or the passion has ebbed away, check to see if you are respecting your groom. God specifically directs wives to be respectful because God knows how important it is to our marriages—including in the bedroom. The key to developing respect is to understand what is respectful behavior and what is not. Many times, I think we as women are oblivious to what our husbands consider disrespectful. If God has called us to respect our husbands, it is vital we learn what that looks like practically. Respect 101 starts in the next chapter.

Challenge

Text your husband "I respect you." Perhaps add a reason why such as, "I respect you because you work hard to keep a roof over our heads," or "I respect you because you are kind to people." Even if you have to dig deep to find a reason, letting him know will be a giant step towards getting your soul mate back. Never forget the passion you once had because God can restore it.

He fashioned the stars into constellations we know by name—Bear, Orion, the Pleiades—and the lights of the southern sky. He does wonderful things, even confounding things, and performs an infinite number of miracles.

- Job 9:9-10 VOICE

Nine

Respect 101

Nevertheless, each husband is to love and protect his own wife as if she were his very heart, and each wife is to respect her own husband.

- Ephesians 5:33 VOICE

Before I took Miss Yurick's Home Economics class in eighth grade, I thought I understood all the nuances of cooking. I know how to sift, whip, fold, fry, baste, boil, blend, sauté, and stir. However, her class quickly revealed I had a lot to learn. I did *not* know how to braise, blanch, coddle, emulsify, mull, reconstitute, or truss. We might think we know the basics when it comes to respect, but let's see if we can learn a few more applications.

Speak in a Pleasant Tone

Even when we are having a bad day, we manage to speak politely to the Safeway checker or to our girlfriend when she calls our cellphone. But when we get into a conversation with our man, snarkiness can creep in. Or as one honest woman told me at a conference I spoke at, "My husband tells me that I can be quite snippy." Our marriages are too important to allow something as simple as our tone of voice to tear down our home. Be intentional about the pitch of your voice—maybe go back to the way you spoke to your man when you were dating and first fell in love. Chances are it was quite pleasant.

Greet Him at the Door

The next time your husband comes home from work or play, greet him at the door. Look him in the eye and say, "I'm glad you are home." Maybe even give him a kiss. This is so simple and yet it says loud and clear to your man, "I respect you." Give him some re-entry time and a chance to unwind before telling him about any problems needing his attention. If our men come home to a nagging, disrespectful wife every day, they will begin to avoid coming home. They will stay at work or play longer, and we will become resentful—the snowball of disrespect and disharmony will begin to roll and pick up speed.

Put Away the White Gloves

If your husband has completed a chore or a task, avoid checking behind him to make sure he did it to your standards. If he loads the dishwasher for you, don't rearrange it—even it if means you can cram in an extra three cups, four bowls and five plates! It doesn't really matter in the end, does it? I promise, if you are a re-arranger, you will find your husband will slowly stop helping you with the dishes to avoid the feeling of disrespect. I recall doing this to my sweet brother-in-law one year when he was visiting from Canada. He was kind enough to offer to do all the dishes after we ate a meal together with a few family members. After he was done doing all the clean-up, I noticed a few dishes still in the sink, so I rearranged the dishwasher to fit them all in. Little did I know how disrespectful that might have felt. I'm learning, and life is sweeter because of it.

Let Him Lead

We all know practice makes perfect, so we need to give our guys a chance to practice leading so they can become great leaders. Husbands will make mistakes along the way, but don't we all? When our guys step out to lead, let them lead. If he says, "Let's clean the garage today," go with it. If he says, "Let's watch the game today," make some snacks. Yes, we have our own ideas, and there is nothing wrong with discussing other possibilities for the day. Be cautious how often we undermine his decisions because of the desire to stick to our *own* agenda. When he sets his foot down, do we find sly ways to get around his choice? Be aware because that maneuver shouts disrespect.

I have heard so many women say they wish their husbands would be the leaders of their home—I said that countless times in my first marriage. Have you ever hoped for that? If so, ask yourself if you have followed his lead when he has made decisions. A leader needs followers and the opportunity to lead. If every time our husbands attempt to make a decision, we question him or go against him, this will take away his desire to lead. Our human nature wants to avoid conflict, so our husbands will naturally pull back from their God-given role as leader if we constantly fight against their choices.

Let your husband lead, and he will eventually become a leader. Check to see if you need to get the spiritual duct tape out and apply sound advice from our brother James.

Understand this, my beloved brothers and sisters.

Let everyone be quick to hear [be a careful, thoughtful listener],

slow to speak [a speaker of carefully chosen words and],

slow to anger [patient, reflective, forgiving];

- James 1:19 AMP

This is not to say we should never express our opinion. However, be slow to speak. Pray about if, when, and how to share that point of view, and when you do, use a respectful tone.

Check Before Making Major Decisions

Marriage is a partnership and a place for mutual respect. Ideally your husband will consult you on major decisions and look for your counsel, and we need to do the same. Are you in the habit of making major decisions without checking with your husband? Your husband should always have a say in big decisions such as where to go for vacation or how to spend a tax return. Even making plans for the weekend should involve a discussion with your husband. If you don't consult him, you run the risk of making him feel disrespected. But when you go to your husband and ask his opinion, this puts a huge check in the respect column which ultimately benefits both of you. He will appreciate being consulted rather than insulted.

Occasionally, the Lord will use us to prevent our husbands from making a mistake, and other times the Lord wants to use our husband's poor choice as a tool to mold him into a man after God's heart. Let's not impede the work God is looking to accomplish. We need to obey the Lord the best we can and leave the results to Him. Remember, we are not called to be our husband's Holy Spirit.

Checking with your husband regarding social decisions is important too. My husband is an introvert, and I am an extrovert. If our social calendar was all about what I want to do, we would be out with friends almost every night of the week. But I know that too much socializing drains my husband and steals his joy, so I always check with him before committing. Because I respect his need for privacy and alone time, he is very generous in his willingness to put entertaining events on the calendar. We have mutual respect for each other which brings a sweet balance. Consider consulting your husband before committing the two of you to anything.

Make Him Feel Competent

Husbands need their wives to support them and make them feel competent to handle their own affairs. Don't *tell* your husband what or what not to do. Build him up by praising him when he does something well.

If your husband has behaviors that are seemingly wrong from your viewpoint, you might need to let him face his own consequences rather than nagging him like a mother hen. We are called to train up a child, not train up a husband! Ask the Holy Spirit to make him aware of certain actions, and you just might find someone else will point out the errant conduct—and the correction won't disintegrate your relationship.

Watch that your reaction to his behavior does not pour gasoline on the fire and make things worse. An acquaintance of mine is known for smacking her husband's shoulder when he does something wrong in public. For example, if he gets in front of her in the buffet line... smack! Or if he takes a piece of cake before the hostess has served dessert... smack! Though his behavior might be considered rude or improper, her disrespect toward her husband is equally as inappropriate and will leave him feeling incompetent and disrespected. Instead, she could build her husband up by praising him about the good things he does rather than henpecking about all the little things. Satan wants us to focus on the petty because his goal is to tear our marriages apart. Don't let him trick you into taking the bait he dangles in front of you.

Fools show their annoyance at once, but the prudent overlook an insult.

- Proverbs 12:16 NIV

Circumstances will arise when a nudge of constructive criticism or piece of advice can and should be delivered by a man's wife. Communicating about various situations can be a blessing to a husband if done correctly. The key is making sure to communicate with a respect-filled tone and good timing. For example, imagine you are both getting ready to attend cousin Ned's wedding and your husband puts on shorts. This might be an opportunity to gently suggest that pants might be more in line with the dress code.

The delivery of the suggestion is key to the acceptance of your proposal. Stating with a smirk on your face, "You are seriously not planning to wear shorts," will not add sweetness to the chocolate cake recipe. Your husband might go into defensive mode and decide to wear a Budweiser tank top to compliment those shorts! Instead, we could say, "I personally love seeing those sexy legs, baby, but I think most of the men might be wearing pants."

Our tone and delivery make a world of difference. And if he decides to wear shorts anyway, don't let that affect the way you treat him the rest of the evening. When we get right down to it, does it really matter if he wears shorts? Or leaves the toilet seat up, the lid off the toothpaste or the towel on the floor?

Let our actions honor our husbands and our Father in heaven and leave the rest to God. The world will not come to an end if my husband wears shorts to a wedding; however, my marriage could slip into the grave if I allow little annoyances to pile up into a huge mound of disrespect. Remember, Satan hates us, and he hates our marriages. He works overtime to bring division, so don't allow him to trick you into falling into one of his traps.

Avoid Mommy Mode

One common area of disrespect happens when we innocently and perhaps unintentionally treat our husbands like we are their mommies. Watch for this one if you have little ones underfoot throughout the day and you are in mommy-mode from sunup to sundown. Without even realizing, we can inadvertently allow our maternal words and actions to spill over into our relationship with our husbands. Our desire might be to help our men, but if in the process we treat them like children, this will come across as disrespectful. Reminding my husband to bring his jacket because it's cold outside or to put his napkin on his knee while at dinner are things I would do to train up a child, not to show respect to the head of my home. Let's decide today not to tell our men what to do, or not to do, as though they are two-year-olds.

Our intentions are often well-meant; we just want to help our husbands. But if my words sound or feel like his mama is talking to him, I need to change my delivery. We shouldn't tell our husbands what to do or how to do it. We are not called to *train up a husband in the way he should go*.

While shopping in Costco a while back, I overheard a confrontation between a young wife and her husband. He was about six feet tall and she was about five-foot two, both with wedding rings on their fingers. With a young boy on one hip and her hand on the other, she sneered at her husband. "It's not that difficult. Do you want the protein bars or not? Use your words!"

My jaw dropped. This young wife had slipped way too deep into Mommy-mode with her words and her tone. Imagine the message she modeled to their young son. It took everything in me not to say to her, "Dear one, unless you want to end up divorced and living the life of a frazzled single mother with your precious young son trying to survive in a broken home, I want to encourage you to apologize to your husband for speaking to him that way." I know it's possible her husband has his own issues. But if we want change in our marriage, we need to clean up our side of the street and pray our husbands will work on theirs. Be aware of what we model to our sons and daughters, too, if you have children. Would we want a daughter-in-law to treat our son the same way we treat our husband?

Mommy-mode can infiltrate the bedroom too. A man can feel sexually repelled by a woman who talks and behaves like his mother all the time. Yikes! Even when it comes to nicknames. Be conscious of how often you call your husband *Daddy*. I know this is normal when kids are around, but make sure you also, at least occasionally, use marriage nicknames like *Baby* or *Honey*. Be aware of the little things that collectively amount to larger concerns. Issues between the sheets can be a result of mothering our husbands.

When we treat our husbands as our lovers and best friends, we will feel more vibrant, alive, and sensual. When we feel sexy, we are more connected to the power of our femininity which enhances our sex life instead of stifling it. We'll talk more about that in the next chapter.

Honor Your Husband's Preferences

Honor your husband's decisions and choices. If he likes to have dinner at five o'clock, do your best to coordinate that even if you prefer to dine closer to six. Prioritizing your husband's preferences shows you respect him, and this will benefit both of you in the long run. He might start to suggest dinner closer to six to love and honor you, but you made the move towards respect and will be blessed for that godly attitude.

Honor His Father and Mother

Don't speak poorly of his mother or father even if he does. The fifth commandment calls us to honor our parents. Chiming in agreement about what a nag his mother is or how boorish his father is goes against God's authority. Even if his mother is the most difficult woman on the planet, do your best to say something nice or nothing at all. I've learned that spiritual duct tape can be very affective!

Since you are all set apart by God, made holy and dearly loved, clothe your-
selves with a holy way of life: compassion, kindness, humility, gentleness,
and patience. Put up with one another. Forgive. Pardon any offenses against
one another, as the Lord has pardoned you, because you should act in kind.
- Colossians 3:12-13 VOICE

Choices as a Homemaker

Something we might not think about as an act of respect is how we dress and keep our home. When we are expecting a friend to come over for a visit, we typically take the time to tidy up, brush our teeth, freshen our lipstick, and maybe even light a couple of candles. How about doing that for the men we made a covenant with God to love, honor and cherish? It doesn't take much time to go that extra mile—we just have to choose to make the effort. We probably used to do that when we were first dating, or as newlyweds, but then the years go by, and we find ourselves not even greeting our husband at the door. Our marriages will reap long-lasting benefits if our husbands feel honored. Do your best to look nice and create an atmosphere that is a haven to come home to. What a wonderful way to demonstrate love and respect to our husbands, and we just might find them more eager to come home.

Disciplining the Children

Another way to ramp up the respect meter is to not take over when our husbands are disciplining the kids. We might *think* our way of correcting is better, but our children need to know that daddy is the head of the house. Unless your husband is abusive in any way, you don't need to intervene as this undermines his authority. He is perfectly capable of handling the situation—even if we think our way is more productive. If you are in the habit of jumping in and micromanaging when your husband takes the lead, force yourself to take a step back. I interfered too often in my first marriage which enhanced the disrespect the boys often showed to their dad. There were times when he was physically abusive, and I *needed* to step in. However, I should have been more prayerful and careful about when and how to intercede. Sometimes our husbands will want our help. But wait for him to give the signal, and then back him up as needed.

Jesus, Take the Wheel

A common complaint from husbands is that wives do too much back-seat driving. If we want to go from the flat egg pancake to the rich, gooey chocolate cake, then we need to stop telling our husbands how to drive. He is perfectly capable—he even has his very own license! Our husbands know what to do behind the wheel, and they feel disrespected when we become their personal DMV instructor telling them to slow down, speed up, or put the turn signal on. When we do this, we are treating our husbands like a fifteen-year-old with a learner's permit. Chances are our husband has had his license as long as we have or maybe even longer. We don't need to tell him where to park or which route to take to get to our destination either. Focus on building your husband up, not on telling him where to go. It might not seem like a big deal to us, but to our men, it's huge. In a survey with men of various ages, I discovered this common theme: A man thinks that if his wife does not trust him to find his way to a set destination, then she probably doesn't really trust him with the important areas like providing for the family or being a good father. What message are we sending?

Undivided Attention

Give your husband your undivided attention when he talks to you. I slipped into the habit of casually checking my phone for emails and texts as my husband talked to me until I caught myself and acknowledged my own rudeness. I don't like it when my husband looks at his phone when I'm speaking to him, so I should show him, and everyone else, the same courtesy. These bad habits slip in and do tiny amounts of damage just like the termites we talked about. We don't notice until the damage has been done and repairs need to be made. Exterminate the rude behavior and save the need for expensive repairs—or expensive marriage counseling.

Caution Against Praising Other Men

Be careful not to excessively praise another man in front of your husband. Going on about another man is a surefire way to bruise your husband's ego. While attending a couple's Bible study several years ago, we were asked to share an example of someone with great faith. One of the wives talked about what an amazing man her son's youth group leader had become. But then she proceeded to go on and on about what a devoted father this young man was, how much he trusted God, how often he read his Bible, how handsome he was, etc. Her husband sat beside her as she bubbled on, and I know the same things could have been used to describe him. You could see the despondency move into his eyes as his wife paid tribute to this other man. Even his body language shouted, "This feels uncomfortable and disrespectful," as he crossed his arms and shifted ever-so-slightly away from his wife. When you have the chance to choose a man to praise, choose your husband or, at the very least, limit the praises for other men. If you have a celebrity crush, be cautious about going on and on about him too. Put yourself in your husband's shoes. What if he was to go on and on about a female co-worker, telling you how organized she is, how well she carries herself, how chic she dresses, how thankful he is to have her as an employee? I know I would not appreciate an abundance of praise being poured onto another woman.

Public Correction

Avoid correcting your guy in public. If your husband is telling a story in a social setting, and he begins with, "About five years ago, Millie and I went to the Grand Canyon," don't jump in and say, "No, Fred, that was eight years ago!" If it's not a tremendously significant detail that needs to be corrected—and they very rarely are—just let it go. Otherwise your man will *hear* you saying, "No dummy, that was eight years ago, not five," even if you didn't mean to come across that way. Corrections are very subtle and very disrespectful. Would we correct our pastor or our father if they were telling a story? Probably not, because it would be impolite; so, let's not correct our husbands either. He is the one-person God specifically tells us to respect, so we need to heed God's counsel.

Allow Him to Speak

When conversing socially, don't jump in and answer questions directed at your husband. Our husbands are fully capable of answering for themselves. In fact, we might learn something new about them if we let them speak for themselves. Pull out that spiritual duct tape because it will come in handy. So often, as women, we use way too many words on our husbands as it is, and if we don't let them speak, we only exacerbate that. If you are in the habit of speaking for your husband, pray that God will help you to be slow to speak, and you might find yourself having a more enjoyable time discussing matters with your mate.

Don't Interrupt

Don't interrupt your husband when he is speaking. Again, God's Word is our guide reminding us to be quick to listen and slow to speak.[54] When our husbands are expressing an opinion or thought, let's turn off our agree/disagree filter. Stop preparing what to say next and instead listen to what he is saying. If you are tempted to interrupt your husband while he is talking, listen for a five-count beat longer. Often times, waiting a few moments gives our men the opportunity to share more than we might have expected, and it could bring clarity to his point of view. When we listen with "new ears," we often gain the connection with our men that we so deeply desire.

Interrupting our husband is like waving a red cape in front of a bull—the nostrils flare and steam comes out of his ears. Initially, he was trying to convey one thought, but if we get him off-track by disrespecting him, in his anger he might end up saying something completely different than he intended. And then we'll wonder how we ended up in an argument. We have to be intentional about avoiding interruption so that we don't become our own worst enemy in the conversation. Let him finish. If you do interrupt your husband, as I have done so many times, quickly apologize so you can diffuse the potential disrespect. "Sorry, baby. I shouldn't have interrupted. Go on." So easy to say, and the apology will make a huge difference in your communication with your man.

Silent But Deadly – Body Language

We all know silence can be deadly. However, our seemingly hushed body language can be yelling disrespect even if we are beginning to master the control of our tongue. Though we might have made great progress in turning off our verbal agree/disagree filter, rolling our eyes while our husband is speaking, is equally as disrespectful as interrupting him with words. Pursing your lips, scowling, or crossing your arms are all dialects that speak volumes. These can be hard habits to break, but let's look to silence them one conversation at a time.

I didn't even realize that over the years I had developed a bad habit of eye-rolling. I was known to do it when I disagreed with my husband, my children, and even co-workers. I needed to own this disrespectful habit and slowly but surely conquer the mannerism. I want the best God has for me, so I am determined to work on the behaviors I bring to my marriage that could cause harm. Holy Eye-rolling does not reflect well on a woman after God's own heart. Ask yourself, "What is my body language saying?" If it's translating into disrespect, start to make a change today.

We can be disrespectful without uttering a word in another way too. Have you ever given your husband "The Look"? You know, the one that has the hashtag #IfLooksCouldKill? Maybe he did or said something that struck you the wrong way, and you shot "The Look" his way. They say a picture can be worth a thousand words—so can a look. We can say a thousand words of disrespect to our husbands in one look of contempt. As wives, we have to be aware of our facial expressions and ask God to fill us with His spirit each and every day so that our faces shine with the light of Jesus. We want to model love and respect to our husbands and to those around us, and the looks we give play a role in that.

If you aren't sure if you are giving off sign-language that spells d-i-s-r-e-s-p-e-c-t, ask your husband. Have a conversation with him. Simply say, "Baby, I want to be more respectful when I communicate with you. Is there anything that I do, verbally or non-verbally, when we converse that makes you feel disrespected?" Then be open to what he might share. Accepting constructive criticism is a sign of maturity, so don't get defensive if your husband has a critique to share.

If you ignore criticism, you will end in poverty and disgrace;

if you accept correction, you will be honored.

- Proverbs 13:18

If you listen to constructive criticism,

you will be at home among the wise.

- Proverbs 15:31

Now that we are more aware of how our body language can inaudibly speak volumes of disrespect, we need to be careful we don't nag silently either. For example, if your husband never seems to help with the dishes, and you do them with a little huff and the purposeful banging of a pot, you are nagging without saying any words. A silent nag here and a silent nag there, here a nag, there a nag, everywhere a nag-nag! You might not be verbally nagging him to help with the dishes, but the message is spoken just the same. Let it go.

Obey God and leave the consequences to Him.

— Charles Stanley. [55]

Try turning your dishwashing time into a time of prayer and praise—which might include asking the Lord to change your husband's heart to want to help you. Or perhaps to change your heart to contentedness while serving your husband in that capacity. Changing your frame of mind can make all the difference.

Remember, Satan is looking to destroy our marriages so don't take the bait that he dangles in front of you to disrespect your husband. Some days the trap is set more often than others. I have to make a conscious effort during some seasons of our marriage to purpose to remain respectful. I know blessing comes through obedience to God's word, so I sidestep the lure and deception that the enemy places in my path and *choose* to walk away from the bait. Be on guard, dear one. Don't take the bait.

Could disrespect spill over into your sexual intimacy? The next chapter answers that question. But first, your challenge.

Challenge

Ask your husband if there are things you do or say that he finds disrespectful. Be ready to receive these constructive criticisms and respond with a teachable heart. I would recommend praying for the right timing and opportunity to discuss this, and then be quick to make any changes he might point out. As you bring respect back into your marriage, you will see your husband's love for you grow.

Ten

Roommates to Soul Mates

My loved ones, let us devote ourselves to loving one another. Love comes straight
from God, and everyone who loves is born of God and truly knows God.

1 John 4:7

Could a lack of respect be stealing the romance and intimacy from your marriage? Why do so many women find that the passion between the sheets fizzles after a few years of matrimony? Sometimes, it's because kids enter the mix, and we are just plain tired and distracted. Sometimes it's because we are getting old. It's tough to feel sexy with Cheerios stuck to the front of your shirt or when Ben-Gay is rubbed on your knees. But there are a few other possibilities worth exploring because when you get right down to it, don't many of us wish that we wanted to make love more often?

After we say, "I do," there are three main camps when it comes to sexual intimacy. The first camp with the most occupied cabins is the one where the husband wants sex all the time, and the wife would be fine holding hands on the way to bed, spooning for a bit, and going to sleep—sex is nice once in a while.

The second camp, which has become a bit more popular in the last decade or so, is filled with wives who want sex more often but have a hard time getting their husbands to join in. The negligee is on, the candles are lit, Spotify love songs are playing, but he's not that interested. You are not alone. Hang on, there's hope. If you are the one making that first move and he is denying you, stay with me as we will discuss this shortly.

The third and most coveted camp is the one where the husband and wife are both equally interested in making love—clothes are flung to the floor with no inhibition, no tension, just red-hot monogamy! If this is where you reside, rejoice! It's an amazing place to live—an area more couples could get a reservation for if they flipped the pages in God's recipe book, followed the directions, and added the right ingredients. Sometimes the Lord does not open up a spot in this camp until certain ingredients get poured into a marriage, so don't dismay if your tent is pitched in one of the first two sites. With God, ALL things are possible. Blessing follows obedience.

As most couples can attest, a good sexual relationship doesn't start when you climb into bed—it is an expression of lives lived in an atmosphere of love, romance and respect. "No lovin' at seven, no heaven at eleven!" For men, this means it's best to woo us, romance us, and make us feel loved *before* reaching to unfasten the bra strap. For women, we need to understand the importance of respect with regards to intimacy: "No respect at seven, no heaven at eleven!"

If we struggle with intimacy and find ourselves lying next to our roommate instead of our soul mate, perhaps we could ignite the passion by pouring heaping cups of respect into our chocolate cake batter. If our husband feels disrespected throughout the day, there will be a chill in the air in our bedroom at night. The snowball of disrespect can roll undetected and gather so much mass that it eventually crushes romance and demolishes desires. If passion is fizzling in your bedroom, it could be because you allowed disrespect to steal the intimacy God wants you to enjoy.

Most men find it nearly impossible to express love and romance to a woman who has a habit of nagging and disrespecting him. Is it true our husbands *will have sex* after experiencing disrespect? Sometimes. However, if you want to *make love* and keep the passion burning or reignite the passion you once had, respect is a key ingredient in the recipe to rekindle intimacy.

Ask the Holy Spirit to show you if you have been critical, cutting, or sarcastic towards your husband. Disrespectful behavior will eventually decrease a man's desire and ability to be tender and romantic. Be intentional about showing him honor throughout the day, and you may find yourself lying next to a new man tonight—not a new husband, but a changed husband. If you and your guy are not on the same page sexually and are not enjoying a passionate sex life, there is hope as long as you keep checking God's recipe and become a doer of His Word.

A husband's masculinity is tied to whether or not he feels admired. When we disparage our spouse, we steal away that masculinity and he may attempt to cover up real or imagined deficiencies by refusing sex. When we don't let our husband be the leader in our home in other areas, chances are he will not take the leadership role in the bedroom either.

Here's a paragraph from Darien Cooper's book *You Can Be the Wife of a Happy Husband*:[56]

"Joan tried to get her husband to go for a medical check-up, feeling his inability to have sex with her was a physical problem. Finally, her husband handed her an article he had clipped from the newspaper. It said, in essence, that a man does not find a woman appealing sexually, if she is constantly bickering or has attacked his masculinity by not allowing him to be the leader, provider, and protector in his home."

Ask God to show you if this is an area that you need to look at.

Another potential culprit for waning passion is a simple health issue. Low libido occurs when testosterone and hormone levels dip as men get older. Chronic disease, medications, and drug use can also wreak havoc on virility. Pray your husband would be willing to go for a medical checkup in order to rule out any of these possibilities.

When a husband does not appear to be interested in sex, another potential culprit is pornography. A staggering percentage of men are addicted to porn as Satan has worked overtime to make cyber-adultery more and more tantalizing, realistic, and accessible. A man hooked on this visual stimulant will find it progressively difficult to make love to his wife. His guilty conscience plays havoc with his mind as he attempts to have sex. "Normal sex" doesn't stimulate him like the twisted online version. Darkness invades the marital bed and leaves filthy tracks. One of the fastest growing arenas of this evil industry are sales of virtual reality (VR) headsets, female robots, and portable lifelike vaginas. The destructive wake of this trend tears hearts and families apart. If you suspect your husband is engaging in pornography, pray. Fast and pray—fervently. Talk to your pastor about how to broach the subject, and seek counsel about the path to take for restoration. Pornography is like cancer to a marriage—death can be imminent if left untreated.

If you are watching pornography, get help, dear one. The enemy thrills at the bondage and shame. But Jesus came to give life in abundance. Don't allow Satan one more second of your life. Our God is a chain-breaking, life-saving, freedom-giving Warrior who will battle for you. Cry out to Him in repentance, and ask Jesus to triumph over this foothold. Step out of the shadows into the light as confession and repentance usher in victory. Put boundaries in place to protect your time and access to the internet. Liberty is on the horizon, sweet sister.

Passion begins in the mind and heart which then spills over into what we say and do. What we say to ourselves about our husbands and what we say directly to our husbands has a huge impact on our intimacy. If you find yourself thinking negative thoughts about your man, take those thoughts captive and replace them with positive ones.

> *Summing it all up, friends, I'd say you'll do best by filling your minds and meditating on things true, noble, reputable, authentic, compelling, gracious— the best, not the worst; the beautiful, not the ugly; things to praise, not things to curse. Put into practice what you learned from me, what you heard and saw and realized. Do that, and God, who makes everything work together, will work you into his most excellent harmonies.*
>
> - Philippians 4:8,9 MSG

We demolish arguments and every pretension that sets itself up against the knowledge of God, and we take captive every thought to make it obedient to Christ.

- 2 Corinthians 10:5 NIV

Let's look at a practical application. If you find your husband's damp towel lying on the floor in the bedroom—again—this thought might pop into your head: "Urrgh, he always leaves his towel on the floor. He treats me like I'm his maid." Has this thought or something similar to it ever popped into your mind? When you get right down to it, this thought is a lie from the enemy, and this enemy wants to tear apart your marriage. Your husband did not toss that towel on the floor ominously thinking, "Muu-ha-ha! I'm going to leave my wet towel on the floor, so my maid/wife has to pick up after me! That'll get her!" He isn't intentionally trying to hurt you. Most men are not multi-taskers by nature. This does not mean they are not intelligent. It simply means men think differently than women. God designed them that way. The husband in this scenario probably thought about what shirt to put on after his shower, and the towel fell to the floor while in transit to the closet.

Therefore, take that negative "maid thought" captive and replace it with something truthful and praiseworthy like this: "I'm thankful my husband has good hygiene and showers. I'm also thankful I have the health and ability to bend down and pick up his towel for him. I want to be the helpmate God designed me to be." Practice replacing negative thoughts with positive ones, and you will usher harmony into your mind and home, and ultimately more passion into your bedroom. Your sex life truly does start in the mind—don't allow the enemy to play mind games with you.

If you meditate on all the things your husband does wrong, eventually you will find yourself married to someone you do not even like. You married your guy because you loved him at one point, so if that love has gone wayward, begin to focus on all the things he does that you love and appreciate. This change in thought pattern will soften your heart toward your husband and can be a key component to reviving passion in the bedroom. One decision at a time; one thought at a time. Decide to respect him in your thought life first.

As you change your thoughts about your husband, change what you verbalize to him, too. After a few years of marriage, it's easy to slowly but surely fall out of the habit of verbally expressing love to our husbands. When we first dated our husbands, we most likely praised them with compliments about how handsome and wonderful they were. "You look so sexy in those 501s" or "I love that blue shirt on you." However, as the months and years go by, we so easily forget to share those positive feelings, and instead we find ourselves saying things like, "Dang, honey, you look like you're six months pregnant" or "Jamie's husband always texts her notes throughout the day with hearts and kisses. All I ever get from you is 'OK.'"

If you meditate on all the things your husband does wrong, eventually you will find yourself married to someone you do not even like.

Instead of building our husbands up, we slowly tear them down. It's very subtle but common in many marriages if we allow the enemy to have his way with our thought life. Our thoughts become our words, our words become our actions, and our actions can tear down our own homes. Be purposeful about building your husband up inwardly and outwardly. After all, you and he are one; so, as the wrecking ball of negative thoughts heads in his direction, you and your sex life will be part of the same demolition.

Disrespect can show up when our men feel like they fall low on our totem pole of priorities. Playing second fiddle time and time again will cause any man to slowly lose the desire to romance his wife—and intimacy dies a slow death.

Picture a pyramid of life's priorities. Jesus should be at the top—our wonderful counselor, patient friend, mighty defender, and sacrificing savior. Next to our love for God, our devotion to our husbands needs to come before dedication to children, grandchildren, jobs, other friendships, hobbies—even involvement in ministries.

Do you put your kids, family, hobbies, or other friendships ahead of your husband? Take time for a recipe check. Remember that God warns us about the enemy who is actively looking to rob, kill, and destroy—often in subtle yet effective ways. Be on the offense rather than the defense, and look for ways to honor, respect, and love your husband with your actions. Resurrecting respect just might rekindle the passion, kick out the roommate, and bring back your soul mate.

Write a note card to your husband that says, "I respect you because ..." Even if there are things your husband has done to steal away your reverence for him, you can think of something you respect in him.

Here are a few examples:

I respect you because you go to work each day and provide for our family.

I respect you because you are so kind to your parents.

I respect you because you are so good at _____.

I respect you because you are such a good father to our kids.

It's not insincere to *model* respect even if you struggle to *feel* respect for your husband. God calls us to respect our husbands, and He won't call us to do something He will not empower us to do. Your heart will catch up with your emotions as you obey God and leave the results to Him.

Eleven

Passion Between the Sheets

Love flares up like a blazing fire, a very ardent flame.
No amount of water can quench love;

- Songs of Solomon 8:6b-7a VOICE

Now that we know disrespect needs to be pulled off the ingredient list of our Chocolate Cake Marriage, what can we pour into the batter instead? I know the last thing we need as women is to add to our to-do list! But what if we could add some things that would bring romance and passion back into our marriage, and possibly free up the time and energy currently wasted on arguments and avoidance? Such an ingredient might be worth a try.

Let's not let Hallmark dictate when and where we can do things to bless or romance our husbands. We don't have to wait until Valentine's Day to rekindle lost passions. Keeping love alive, or resurrecting old desires, can be done if we get intentional and creative. Sometimes, when there are lots of past hurts and baggage involved, reviving desire can take perseverance, but when God is for you, who can be against you?[57]

Here's a list of ideas to rekindle intimacy or to enhance the passion you might already be enjoying. Grab a highlighter and challenge yourself to do at least five of these in the next month. Some of the ideas literally take five seconds to do, so it will be easy if you are willing.

Choose things you know would bless your husband, not things you wish he would do for you. For example, you might think it would be romantic for your husband to send a bouquet of Mylar balloons to your workplace with a love note and ribbon attached, but would that same bouquet bless him? I think my husband would pretend he didn't know who "Michelle" was if I sent a bouquet to his office! That is not his love language. However, if I showed up in the bedroom with a ribbon and balloon tied to me? Now we're talking! Put yourself in your husband's shoes and pick things he would like even if it means stepping outside your comfort zone.

Some of these ideas might be too outlandish for you. For example, you might not want to show up at your front door wearing nothing but an overcoat, ring the doorbell, and wait for your husband to come to the door. Though I guarantee most husbands would be over the moon with excitement if their wife was willing to be that daring and sexy. Challenge yourself, and you'll lift your marriage out of the rut and onto a new, exciting track.

Here are some ideas to try. Highlight away!

- **Set reminders to do special things.** Set reminders on your calendar for five random days of the month—perhaps on the 5th, 10th, 15th, 20th and 25th and let these be cues to do something special for your husband. I don't know about you, but the days and months seem to fly by. If something is not written on my calendar, it "ain't gonna happen." When my husband and I were newlyweds, I did not need any reminders to do special things, but as the years go by, though I am still madly in love, I can forget to do special things for him. Don't let that rut get its groove on!

- **Greet your husband at the door when he comes home.** This is on our respect list too, because it is worth repeating. When we greet our men, we demonstrate honor and send the message that we don't take them for granted. Our husbands want to feel like the "King of the Castle," so when we greet our men with a kiss and show appreciation they are home, we will stir passion back into our chocolate cake. When he is on his way home, consider a quick change out of the grey sweats and pony tail into something more appealing. When I know a friend is coming over, I usually tidy up the house, light a couple candles, brush my teeth and put on fresh lipstick. Shouldn't I do the same thing when I know the man I made a vow to love and honor is on his way home? Too many husbands are staying later at the office or longer on the links because the home front feels chaotic and uninviting. Let's be wives that our husbands look forward to coming home to with a smile on our faces, a warm hello, and perhaps even a Tic-Tac popped into our mouths.

- **Set up the coffee machine.** Before you head to bed, set up the coffee pot with a little Post-It note saying, "Good morning. I love you!" So easy, and what a beautiful way for your husband to start his day. If he's more of a protein shake guy, set up the blender with a few of his shake ingredients next to it. You might even find him setting a treat out for you once in a while.

- **Give him an unexpected neck rub.** Just come up behind his chair, put your hands on his neck—not around his neck—on his neck! ☺ Give him a little neck rub, back scratch, or scalp massage. That feels nice. If your husband's love language is physical touch, a massage is a particularly powerful way to fuel passion. Sometimes the Lord will nudge you to do this when you would rather wring his neck instead. This is when the rubber meets the road, and you need to decide on obedience or disobedience. Just remember, God always blesses obedience.

- **Squeeze his hand three times.** You'll have to explain this one beforehand, but it's a fun one—great for kids and grandkids, too. When you are somewhere you can't talk, such as sitting in church, at the movie theater, or even while watching TV on the couch—hold his hand and squeeze three times for *I...love... you.* He will always know what you are saying when he feels those three squeezes.

- **Pick up his favorite treat.** When you are shopping for groceries, get a little something that is your husband's favorite—maybe a bag of pistachio nuts, a Snickers bar, or the pastrami he really likes—just to show you're thinking about him. Buying an extra item takes very little time but will be one more step on the path to passion.

- **Write your love story.** Write the love story of how you met your husband and what your courtship was like. Talk about the feelings you had when you first saw him, what attracted you to him, and perhaps how he proposed. Add as many details as you can. Have the pages printed and bound—Kinkos or Staples can do this for you. You can include some ticket stubs, photos, or other mementos if you wish. The booklet will make a nice keepsake—perhaps even an heirloom. If you have children, it might be fun for them to know some details about your story and how you met and fell in love. If for some reason you don't want anyone to know those details—let alone have them in print—then don't highlight this one. This is all about blessing your husband and ultimately your marriage.

- **Put a Valentine basket together**—Even in April or October! Don't let Hallmark dictate what days to celebrate. Include a love letter, a couple of candles, sparkling cider, some of his favorite munchies, maybe even the negligée from your wedding night—dig that thing out of the back of your sock drawer and shake the dust off if you need to! Lord knows we don't really need to put those things on—simply holding it up can be all that's necessary. You could even put the basket at the front door, ring the door bell, and run! Be silly. Sometimes the reason our marriages fall into ruts is because we get too serious and forget to be playful and laugh with each other. Pinch your husband's booty while walking through the frozen food aisle on your next grocery run—pretending you're still dating can smooth that rut right out!

- **Make a memory together**—just the two of you. Make memories with family and friends, but be intentional about making romantic memories that involve only the two of you. Book a horse-drawn carriage or gondola boat ride if those are available in your city. If your budget is a bit tight, go for a moonlit walk around your neighborhood or pack a basket with food and candles for a picnic in your backyard or living room. Once we packed a blanket, warm gloves, and hot chocolate to watch a Christmas boat parade together—it didn't cost a penny, but we will always remember snuggling together in the cold December air.

- **Turn the lights down at dinner and light a candle.** Even mac 'n cheese with the kids seems more romantic by candlelight. It's all about creating a mood and doing something other than the "same old same old." Use your fancy dinnerware and chargers. Life is short—don't wait for special occasions to make things special.

- **Interview family and friends on video.** Video family and friends sharing why they love and appreciate your husband, or what their favorite memory is with him. If you have children, get them in on this one, and your mother-in-law too. Invite whoever is willing to get in front of the camera—maybe even a neighbor or a favorite coworker. Everyone likes to hear nice things said about themselves, so make that happen for your husband. We tend to take the time to prepare these videos for funerals, but why not arrange for your husband to hear those nice thoughts while he's alive and well?

- **Frame a picture of the two of you** and place it in a prominent position in your home. How many of us have 39 pictures of the kids and family all around the house, but not one of our guys? Maybe it's time for a nice selfie of the two of you.

- **Email or text your husband a couple times a day.** Text short notes that you are thinking about him, or tell him that he's sexy, or a good father. Anything to boost his confidence. Do not be offended if his reply doesn't measure up to your expectations. You might send a heartfelt text with emoticons and romantic words and receive a response that reads, "Cool." Be okay with that—expectations can equal future resentments, so don't expect him to reply with the same level of communication. For many men, long prose is simply outside their comfort zone. Go to Google images and type in "I love my husband," and you will find hundreds of images you can copy and paste into an email or text. You can also send him a YouTube video of a favorite song that will bless him or bring back a great memory.

- **Tell him, "I'm glad I married you!"** Or "I love doing life with you!" This one doesn't cost a nickel but just might be the most valuable. Perhaps you and your husband have been through more valleys than peaks, and he might need to know you are still glad you married him. Tell him.

- **Give him a jar of green M&Ms.** No one knows exactly who started the urban legend, but back in the '70s it was purported that green M&Ms act as an aphrodisiac. The idea took on such a life of its own that Mars

Candy sells bags of green M&Ms for Valentine's Day. What better treat to use to get you in the mood than chocolate, so go with it. I'm sure your husband will share with you!

- **Warm his towel.** When your husband is in the shower, steal his towel, place it in the dryer for a couple of minutes, then bring it back when it's nice and warm and fluffy. A side note for this one: Do not get distracted between the taking of the towel and the replacing of the towel! Otherwise this maneuver will backfire, and your husband will be standing naked and cold in the shower stall wondering what in the world happened to his towel. ☺

- **Burn a CD or make a play list** of all your special songs. This makes a great mood enhancer. It's amazing how a song can take you back to a special time and memory.

- **Randomly hide a bunch of love notes.** I hope you choose to do this one as it has lasting blessings. All you need is lipstick and a pack of Post-It notes. Apply your signature shade and kiss a whole bunch of Post-it notes. Write love messages next to your kiss on each one, such as "You're so sexy," "Thank you for all you do," "I love you," and "I'm glad I married you"—be creative. Place each note in a random location: in his sock drawer, on the back of his car's sun visor, inside the book he's reading, inside his favorite snack bag, under his pillow, in the meat drawer of the fridge, etc. You never know when he will find each one—it could be months from now. He might find one the morning after you had an argument, and it will be the thing to break the ice and get you back on the right track. He might even find one in his briefcase or glove compartment on the same day another woman flirts with him. There are women after our husbands, and these days these seductresses are very aggressive. The enemy wants nothing more than to divide and separate us from our husbands, and Satan will use all kinds of tactics. We need to be on guard for ways to protect our marriages—one of these ways is to build our husbands up so that they would never dream of cheating on us. Help to fend off the fiery darts of temptations from the enemy by reminding your husband that his wife adores him.

- **Bring your husband breakfast in bed.** Again, only highlight this one if it would bless your husband. This is nearly impossible for me to do as my husband literally gets up before the roosters as he is a "get up and go" kind of guy. Breakfast in bed would not be something that he would enjoy. I've learned that offering to make him lunch while he is working in the yard or bringing him his favorite snack while he's watching the game is more appreciated. Use your imagination, and tweak these suggestions to match what makes your husband tick.

- **Write "I love you" on the bathroom mirror** so he will see it when he wakes up in the morning. The first time I did this, I wrote the words on the mirror using the "free gift with purchase" tube of lipstick from my favorite make-up counter—you know, that shade of neon orange that no one would ever wear, but it's free! Well, God bless my sweet man—he reciprocated with a sweet note written on my side of the bathroom mirror. However, when he reached into my make-up drawer to find a writing utensil, he grabbed my favorite Nordstrom splurge lipstick, Mystic Mauve, at sixteen bucks a tube. Eeeeek! All that was left was a little stump of whale fat. However, to this day, he does not know he ruined that tube of lipstick. He would never write on my mirror again if I had griped and moaned to him, "Seriously! You used my Mystic Mauve? You know that's the one I always use!" We can be our own worst enemy and sabotage romantic possibilities when we point out our husbands' shortcomings.

Oh, and I have since switched to using a dry erase marker for writing on the bathroom mirror—works great, washes off easily, and avoids any lipstick catastrophes!

- **Don't criticize him if he misses the mark**—Be thankful he's at least trying. If your husband doesn't think ahead to make reservations for Valentine's Day dinner, and you end up sitting on a bench for an hour and a half waiting to hear "Smith, party of two," don't harp on him for not making reservations—it's not going to change a thing. Just enjoy the time together. And make sure your body language isn't shrieking, "How could you?" Simply be happy he's with you, sit on the bench, hold his hand, and kiss him. Turn the time waiting for your table into a time of romance, and enjoy his company. The Lord allowed it, so make the best of it.

- **Put toothpaste on his brush, too.** If you are first to the bathroom, put toothpaste on your husband's toothbrush. When I first heard this idea from a girlfriend, I didn't think it was very romantic, but she explained how much it had blessed her marriage one particular night. She and her husband had been fighting that evening and could not seem to get past the conflict. When she headed upstairs to get ready for bed, she saw her toothbrush sitting next to the sink with toothpaste already applied. The small act of kindness nudged her toward her husband to give him a hug and say she was sorry for the skirmish. He embraced her, and they listened to God's instruction to not let the sun go down on their anger.

> *Don't go to bed angry. Don't give the Devil*
> *that kind of foothold in your life.*
> *- Ephesians 4:26b-27 MSG*

> *And "don't sin by letting anger control you."*
> *Don't let the sun go down while you are still angry,*
> *for anger gives a foothold to the devil.*
> *- Ephesians 4:26-27*

We just never know when these random gestures will guard against the devil getting a foothold in our marriages. Do not forget that we have an enemy who is out to destroy the oneness we have with our husbands—one onslaught at a time. We need to be vigilant to guard our hearts and homes.

- **Splurge on great tickets**—not to the ballet YOU want to see but to an event your husband would love to attend. Make sure the expense is within your budget and, if he likes surprises, try to surprise him.

- **Make a "He loves me, He loves me" flip calendar.** Chapter Five challenged you to create this keepsake. Keep 3x5 cards close at hand for a few days and write down thirty-one things he does that makes you feel special or blessed. Once you have completed the cards, punch holes in the top of the cards and tie with ribbon. Now you have a little flip calendar reminding you of the good in your husband.

This is a great tool for a couple of reasons. First, we focus on the good things our husbands do. We can have elephant memories for all the bad habits and struggle to reflect on their positive traits. Reminding yourself of the good is particularly important if you seem to only remember things that annoy you. If you are in a difficult period in your marriage, you might have to reminisce about things he used to do for you. You married him for a reason, so think hard and you will be able to come up with a list.

Second, if you show the flip calendar to your husband, he will see firsthand what encourages you. He might not realize that putting gas in your car or locking the house up at night is such a blessing. We are told to think about things that are pure and lovely, so don't allow your mind to wander down the trail of reminders about the things he neglects. Focus on the good and pray about the bad. Ruth Bell Graham advised, "Tell your mate the positive, and tell God the negative. [58] You might find your husband will do items on your list more often. If your man is physically unable to do what he used to do for you, build him up by reflecting on anything he does that's positive, even if it's just the way he smiles at you in the morning.

- **Mail a love letter to your husband at work, or even to your own house.** Don't wait until Valentine's Day to send him a romantic card. The next time you are buying a birthday card for a friend, pick up a card that says, "I love you." Spritz perfume on the inside and seal the envelope with a kiss.

- **Put freshly baked cookies or a breakfast muffin in his car.** Place a treat in his car at night with a note that he'll find as he heads off to work the next morning. How easy is that? And what a great way for your husband to start his day. A little hint—cookies or muffins—are not the only thing you can leave in the car—hanging a sexy pair of underwear from the rearview mirror will start your hubby's morning off right. If this is too daring for you, do it anyway! And if you don't own a sexy pair of underwear, it's time to get a pair.

- **Hold hands and kiss in public.** I only have a few friends who kiss or hold hands with their husbands in public—and these couples happen to have strong marriages. Did you used to hold hands when you were dating? Bring romance back to your marriage even if you've been married for over fifteen, thirty, or forty years. Some men and women don't like PDA [Public Displays of Affection], but if you kissed and held hands early in your relationship, get back into the habit. Be intentional about having a Chocolate Cake Marriage.

- **Prepare his favorite meal.** Get the cookbook out and create his favorite dish. Set the table with chargers, candles, and cloth napkins. Don't wait for a special occasion to do something out of the ordinary.

- **Hide a love note in his suitcase.** If your husband goes on a trip, even just an overnighter, tuck a note into his suitcase or toiletries bag. Know that it's not easy out there on the road—it's lonely, and temptations abound baiting our guys along the way. A love note from you will brighten his day and remind him that his devoted wife is waiting for him at home. Go one step further and attach the note to the sexy underwear that used to hang from the rearview mirror—that will really make him feel appreciated!

- **Set the ambiance.** Spritz perfume on your sheets, and light candles in anticipation of your husband coming to bed. We need to be the aggressor in the bedroom sometimes so step out of the rut and spark the passion. (We'll talk more about making the first move in the next chapter.)

- **Take a photo of your underwear!** Snap a picture of a pair of your sexiest underwear. Make a creative screenshot as though you are posting on Instagram, but this one is just for your man. Position a sexy piece of lingerie on your pillow with a candle in the background and text it to him—no caption necessary.

- **Take a bath together.** Light candles, queue up romantic music, and relax together. Make the effort to do this even once a year—this is much more memorable and romantic than binge watching Netflix on the tube. If you have kids, remember to lock the bathroom door.

- **Join him unexpectedly in the shower!** Getting naked with the lights on and stepping into the shower might be way outside your comfort zone, but you can do it. Just tell yourself, "I'm jumping out of this rut!" Come on, sweet sister, you can. Be strong and courageous.[59]

- **Go to bed wearing nothing but your favorite pair of pumps.** Or if you are really brave, step in front of the TV wearing nothing but your favorite boots! Put a whole new twist on the phrase, "He shoots, he scores!" I did this several years ago and my husband still talks about it.

Start to practice a few of these ideas and nudge your marriage out of the world of mundane and back into the passionate relationship you desire. You may be thinking: "I already do so much. Why do I have to be the one to try to bring passion back? When is it his turn to write the note or rub the neck?" I understand the pain and frustration behind these statements. If your husband is not loving you as Christ loves the church, he is missing God's call to him. But if we want the Chocolate Cake Marriage, we need to consider WWJD—what would Jesus do? He tells us to die to self, and to love and respect our husbands—even if our husbands are not living up to their call. God has designed our walk with Him to make us more like Jesus. Sometimes God allows us to be in a difficult marriage to practice dying to self which in turn makes us more like Christ. Blessings come from obedience. Believe that, dear one. It's truth.

Keep in mind this concept that was coined so perfectly by author Kristen Welch:

The uncomfortable truth of doing what God tells us is this: It's going to cost something—pride, time, money, bravery. But the reward of stepping into the unknown far outreaches and outlasts the price you have to pay.[60]

One more reminder...

Love me when I least deserve it because that is when I really need it.

– Swedish Proverb

In the next chapter, we'll talk more about getting brave when it comes to S-E-X. But first, your challenge.

Challenge

Choose one thing from the list in this chapter, and do it TODAY. Let's be careful not to have expectations about our husband's response to whatever we choose to do—just look to bless him, and leave the rest to God. Remember, we serve a God of miracles.

Twelve

Honey, I've Got a Headache

Your navel is perfectly formed like a goblet filled with mixed wine.
Between your thighs lies a mound of wheat bordered with lilies.

- Song of Solomon 7:2

Wow! That's pretty racy talk, yet it's straight from the Chocolate Cake Recipe book. God designed sex in the confines of marriage for a purpose. Making love is meant to be a passionate, pleasurable way for a husband and wife to experience intimacy and express their love. Yes, making babies can be part of the plan. Equally important is the pleasure and oneness sex should bring to the relationship.

I don't know about you, but during my childhood, our family didn't talk about sex—at all. Not even about the birds and the bees having sex. My first recollection of introduction to the world's view of sex happened when I was about eight years old. My brother and I stayed at a friend of my parents one night, and we were left in the care of a local teenage babysitter while the adults attended a social event. At one point in the evening, someone flipped the TV station to the Playboy Channel—the soft porn channel of the seventies. I remember wondering, "What are they doing?"

Home sick with a fever, I missed the sex education talk in elementary school. On top of that, I was molested as a child for several years by a cousin, and then again as a teenager by a rather large NFL player whose child I babysat. Sex became a tricky subject. In my mind, intimacy had a negative connotation as it seemed somewhat taboo, dirty, and illicit. If sex conjures up some of those same feelings in you, bear with me, dear one, because God has a plan.

It's okay to pray to God about sex.

He can make you new in your sexuality. He declares us a new creation in Christ. God can wash away the bad and replace the negative feelings and emotions with good. He promises this in Isaiah when He declares:

> *To all who mourn in Israel, he will give a crown of beauty for ashes, a*
> *joyous blessing instead of mourning . . .*
> - Isaiah 61:3a

It's okay to pray to God about sex. If you struggle in this area, ask God to heal your pain and restore your innocence—one wound at a time. Then, wait and watch the restoration begin. He is faithful and can make you truly anew in Him.

> *For we are God's masterpiece. He has created us anew in Christ*
> *Jesus, so we can do the good things he planned for us long ago.*
> - Ephesians 2:10

Because God created sex, it's no wonder Satan tries to destroy it. One of the good things God planned for us long ago is to have great sex with our spouse! It's time to consult the recipe so we can savor the chocolate. After all, it's been said that sex is like chocolate—you don't have to be in the mood to enjoy it.

And if this still makes you a bit uncomfortable to talk about, let's look again at what God's Word has to say.

> *How beautiful are your sandaled feet, O queenly maiden. Your*
> *rounded thighs are like jewels, the work of a skilled craftsman.*
> *Your navel is perfectly formed like a goblet filled with mixed wine.*
> *Between your thighs lies a mound of wheat bordered with lilies.*
> *Your breasts are like two fawns, twin fawns of a gazelle.*
> - Song of Songs 7:1-3

Yes ... there is "a mound of wheat," right? I'm not sure what the border of lilies is—perhaps cellulite! But that navel is apparently perfectly formed. God has no problem discussing sex and intimacy, so we shouldn't either. Let's embrace the subject and talk about it so we can have the intimate relationship with our husband that God desires.

With that said, I want to dispel two myths. First, sex is not a four-letter word. Nope. S-E-X, only three. God Himself created this physical act to be enjoyed in the marital bed. Sex is meant to be pleasurable and satisfying, as well as to reflect the oneness of marriage.

Second, the key to a man's heart is not through his stomach. Nope.

That is something your father wanted you to believe. Some studies show that a sexual thought runs through a man's mind every eighteen seconds! I am amazed by that. No wonder most men can't multi-task. So, the reality is that many of our husbands, not all, but the majority, are sex fiends. Women on the other hand are often tired by the end of the day and might just want to snuggle up on the couch rather than hop into the marriage bed. What are we to do? We need to check God's recipe.

Remember, God created sex, and it is a GOOD thing! Satan has tried to convince us that an exciting sex life is dirty and licentious or that sex is only for making babies. Yes, God created sex for propagating, but He also meant it to be exciting and enjoyable for a married couple.

Song of Solomon resembles a steamy love letter between two young married lovers and, along with other Scriptures, speaks beautifully and specifically about sex in marriage. In this book, the husband tells his wife her hair is like a "flock of goats" and her nose is like "the tower of Lebanon." These may not be the romantic words we want whispered in our ears, but in ancient days, those were passionate phrases. Filled with scenarios depicting the sexual desires between a husband and wife, Song of Solomon is a sensuous and exhilarating book.

Back to our question: What are we to do if our husbands want sex all the time, whereas, we might be content holding hands and cuddling?

Most men have large amounts of testosterone running uncontrollably through their veins—this keeps their libido fired up and sex on the brain. They can't help that. God made them this way. They are not perverts or sex-crazed— they are healthy men just the way their Creator made them. Men are also very visually-oriented. We can take a sock off, and they get turned on. Oh baby! Perhaps that toe was the only skin they've seen in a while.

Our husbands want to see us naked, but too many of us have a *Magic Closet* installed in the master bedroom. If this scenario sounds familiar, you might be unaware you have one. It's time to turn in for the night, so you both head to the master bedroom to get ready for bed. At this point, the husband, most likely with sex on his mind, is hoping to catch a glimpse of his naked wife knowing she will undress to put on her night clothes. However, she unceremoniously steps into the *Magic Closet*, and saunters out dressed head to toe in her flannel jammies—his hope dashed. He came so close to seeing skin, but he's left with nothing more than wondering if perhaps tomorrow will bring a small flash of his wife's birthday suit.

Genesis 2:25 (NET) says, *The man and his wife were both naked, but they were not ashamed.*

God designed us this way in the beginning—wouldn't it be nice to delete shame from our mind? We need to ask the Lord to help us remove the indignity many of us feel.

If you struggle getting naked in front of your husband, ask the Lord to help you and heal you. Since the time we first walked by fashion magazines in the grocery checkout line, the covers taunted us that our bodies are either too fat or too thin, our butts are too big or too small, and our breasts are too round or too flat. Even professional fashion models give testimonies that they don't feel pretty. These are women who are paid thousands of dollars to model *because* they are beautiful, and yet the enemy convinces them they don't measure up. We need to replace the lies with truth and get comfortable in our own skin. God ordains us daughters of the King and says we are beautifully and wonderfully made.[61] When your husband isn't home, walk around your bedroom wearing only underwear. As you get comfortable with that, try just a robe with nothing on underneath and the belt undone. Next, drop the robe. Then let your husband see you partially undressed, even if you initially just remove your top in front of him. Baby steps. Work your way to feel comfortable completely nude before him—with the lights on. You are a new creation in Christ and your husband loves you—he wants to see you naked. Jiggly parts and all. Women are typically not visual creatures, but we shouldn't begrudge our husbands' desire to see our bodies, because that is the way God designed them.

> *May your fountain, your sex life, be blessed by God;*
> *may you know true joy with the wife of your youth.*
> *She who is lovely as a deer and graceful as a doe—*
> *as you drink in her love, may her*
> *breasts satisfy you at all times.*
> - Proverbs 5:18, 19 VOICE

Okay, so in some cases, our husbands want to "hook up," and we are wiped out from a long day at work, or from chasing toddlers and changing diapers, or from caring for an elderly parent. What do we do? Time to check the ingredients and directions—and make the decision to create a Chocolate Cake Marriage.

1 Corinthians 7:4-5 VOICE tells us:

> *In marriage neither the husband nor the wife should act as if his or her body is private property—your bodies now belong to one another, and together they are whole. So do not withhold sex from one another, unless both of you have agreed to devote a certain period of time to prayer. When the agreed time is over, come together again so that Satan will not tempt you when you are short on self-control.*

These are God's words, not mine. They come straight from the recipe book. When our husbands make a move on us and we are not in the mood, do we say, "Not tonight, honey, I have a headache. *Let's pray.*" That might sound a bit much to get on our knees and pray each time we deny each other, but the recipe makes the directive clear. On the other hand, we can get into the habit of simply saying "no," and then we *don't* pray, and we *don't* come together again. And Satan has a field day tearing our marriage apart—one denial at a time.

As the verse declares, unless we obey God's Word, Satan will tempt us because of our lack of self-control. Part of the reason why the pornography industry flourishes is our refusal to obey 1 Corinthians 7:4-5. Too many women are saying "no" to their husbands night after night, and then their men are tempted to indulge in pornography as their sexual outlet. If your husband battles with pornography, you can help him conquer the addiction by obeying God's Word. I'm not saying pornography is our fault—nor can a husband blame his decision to watch porn on his wife. However, Scripture does tell us that if we deny our husbands, we are opening the door to Satan and temptation. Let's stop aiding and abetting the enemy with his tactics to tear down our marriages. Of course, the edict applies when husbands deny their wives as well. Female pornography is one of the fastest growing veins of that industry—and Christians are definitely not immune.

A spouse's body is co-owned with their mate. Through obedience and self-control, we need to give our husbands an all-access pass. Do not deny him, dear one. Trust God with this instruction, and you will be one step closer to enjoying the chocolate cake.

I find it interesting that our enemy, Satan, does *everything* he can to get us to have sex *before* marriage. And then works at doing *everything* he can to get us *NOT* to have sex after marriage! We can help defeat the enemy by trusting and following God's recipe for our marriage.

In the book, *Becoming One: Planning a Lasting, Joyful Marriage*, Don Meredith writes:

"God steps boldly to the point, finishing any fainthearted commitment to the sexual relationship once and for all. My body is not mine, but my mate's. I am here to please. Hereafter, to demand rights over my body is to disagree with God's instruction. God makes sex a sacrificial act that is redemptive, in that it gets my eyes off my needs and onto the needs of my mate."[62]

Wow! Maybe hearing a statement like that is easy stuff for you. If you enjoy making love with your husband, giving your body to your mate is a delight. I rejoice that I am blessed to live in this camp as there are wonderful amenities! But for some, saying yes to each of your husband's sexual advances is a challenge, so seeking God for strength to obey is critical. For our marriages to survive and have abundant life, we need to be there for our husbands physically. Eventually, if not immediately, you will be blessed abundantly for your obedience.

We are not to deny our husbands. Feeling too tired or "not in the mood" are excuses that get in the way of the Chocolate Cake Marriage. God says we need to say "yes" to our husbands, and God always has our best in mind. Always.

Now, hopefully, your man will be considerate and understanding if you truly do have a headache or have been up all night with a sick baby or ailing parent. "Mutual consent and taking time to pray" comes in to play at this point.

Let's decide to trust God with this Scripture. If we deny our husbands, we are not following the chocolate cake recipe that leads to a beautiful, delicious end result. Denial is disobedience and will flatten our marriage cake as much as leaving out the eggs and baking soda would do to a real cake. This verse flies in the face of the women's movement that is so pervasive in our culture today. Women march with signs declaring "My body is mine. Hands off." Yes, our bodies are ours, and *no one* but God and our husbands have any right to it. But, we can't deny that God does tell us that our husbands do have rights to their wives' bodies—and vice versa.

> *Let's decide to trust God with this Scripture.*

Saying yes can take courage and self-discipline—especially if a habit has developed of coming to bed with your flannel jammies up to your chin and rolling over to go right to sleep. We can be quick to obey God when He says, "Thou shall not steal" or "Thou shall not kill," but are you willing to obey Him when He says, "Thou shall not turn over and pretend you are asleep?"

Imagine if your child or a family member's little one told you he or she was hungry? *You* might not be in the mood to eat, and you might even be too tired to make a meal, but you will prepare that child something because you love him or her. Let's do the same for our husbands. We might not be hungry for sex, and we might be too tired and not in the mood, but let's make love with our husbands because their appetite is craving us. Denying him hurts us in the long run. Many wives spend more energy on the denial process than if they would have just made love with their man. Let's be real—sometimes sex can be over in five minutes. Just say yes and be blessed.

Keep in mind promiscuous women are on the prowl for our husbands and will attempt to seduce them. We need to be wise, courageous women who diligently protect our marriages by obeying God's instructions.

> *Wisdom will pluck you from the trap of a seductive woman, from the enticing propositions of the adulteress...*
> - Proverbs 2:16 VOICE

God tells us not to deny our husbands for a reason, so let's decide right now to listen to His instruction; disobedience to God's Word is a sin.

> *Remember, it is sin to know what you ought to do and then not do it.*
> - James 4:17

And in case we think, no one will know and it doesn't really matter, God also says our sin *will* eventually find us out.

But if you fail to do this, you will be sinning against the LORD;

and you may be sure that your sin will find you out.

- Numbers 32:23 NIV

Not that God watches over us looking to zap us if we make a wrong move. He loves and adores us and remembers our sin no more.[63] But He also knows what will give us life more abundantly. Much like a father who tells his little girl to not play in the street, he knows that she will have a longer more enjoyable life if she avoids a collision with an automobile. All of God's instructions have our best in mind.

Back to the bedroom. Have you and your husband ever both flopped into bed after a busy day of kids and chores and soccer practices and more chores? Or after a long day of work and traffic and errands, he says, "Man, I am tired. I am ready for a good night sleep." So, you think, "Ah, me too, I am exhausted. Time to fluff my pillow and start counting sheep." You both snuggle in for the night, lights out, eyes closed, and you are drifting off to sleep—and then you suddenly feel something. He and all his manliness have made their way over to your side of the bed. But, he just said he was tired! Why is he making a move?

Many women in this scenario might want to cry out, "I thought you were tired?!" But that would be a form of denial, so we need to put that spiritual duct tape over our mouth and feel blessed that our husbands want to make love with us. God made men different from women in many ways, and one of those ways is that sex can serve as a Tylenol PM for our men—enabling them to relax and go to sleep. How many of us can vouch for that? After you make love, you are staring at the ceiling and he is snoring. Don't begrudge your man for this; it is the way God wired him. He just popped a Unisom!

We also need to be cautious about the mentality, "You got it last night, pal. Tonight is my night off." This will ring loud in our men's ears and can tear down their self-esteem. Remember 1 Corinthians 7:5b VOICE: "*... come together again so that Satan will not tempt you when you are short on self-control.*" The enemy does not sleep and is vigilant about finding opportunities to bring discord. Not tonight, Satan!

The most effective way to show our husbands we love them is to demonstrate we care about them and desire to make love with them. Notice the word *desire*. Not rolling over with a huff, "Oh, fine, I'll do it. Hurry up and get it over with and let me know when you're done." If we act like a starfish, we just might be treated like one. Participate in making love, and fan the flames of passion.

Let's say after reading this chapter you decide to make tonight the night. You get bold and brave and light candles in the bedroom, turn on sexy mood music, and put on that little number from Victoria's Secret that was stuffed in the back of your underwear drawer. You spray on perfume, pop a breath mint, and wait for him to come through the bedroom door. He finally comes in, looks at you, and says, "Not tonight, honey, I'm super tired and just want to go to sleep."

Ugh. Wouldn't you feel rejected, hurt, and even humiliated? You put yourself out there, and he turned you down. You feel rejected. Unwanted. Undesirable. Please know this is exactly what we do to our husbands when we turn down their advances. They feel rejected. Unwanted. Undesirable. Sometimes we forget that our husbands feel these emotions too. Now hopefully they didn't get all dolled up for us—that could be a whole other chapter! But rejection hurts no matter the form and will slowly chip away at our relationships leaving us with that dry, brittle, ugly cake. Don't disregard the carefully laid out instructions in the recipe.

Proverbs 5:19 TLB says, *Let her breasts and tender embrace satisfy you. Let her love alone fill you with delight.*

The wife in this verse is described as tender, satisfying and delightful. Let's concentrate on making our sex life a satisfying experience for our husbands—which in turn will make sex fulfilling for us too.

We also need to be the aggressor sometimes. Most men love when their wives make the first move. In Song of Solomon 7:11-12, the wife says to her husband, *"Come, my love, let us go out to the fields and spend the night among the wildflowers. Let us get up early and go to the vineyards to see if the grapevines have budded, if the blossoms have opened, and if the pomegranates have bloomed. There I will give you my love."* In this scene, we witness the wife making the first move. This lets her husband know that she desires him—not simply to appease him sexually, but to demonstrate she actually yearns for *him* and wants to be *one* with him.

I love when my husband brings me flowers. It makes me feel special—yes, one of my love languages is gifts. What if instead of bringing me flowers, he handed me our Visa card and said, "Here, baby, go up to Triple A Flowers and pick yourself out an arrangement." Hmmmm, I can do that. I will still have a beautiful bouquet of flowers to enjoy. They will still sit on the kitchen table and look pretty and smell nice. However, buying them for myself won't *mean* the same because my husband did not make the effort to bring them to me—I had to go get them. The same is true in-between the sheets. He can come and "get it" so to speak, and we will still enjoy making love. There will still be a pleasurable union, but because he had to "go get it," the act of love won't mean as much. Many husbands will find sex more meaningful and satisfying if their wives "bring it to them" now and then. We might think, how hard is it for my husband to bring me flowers once in a while? Well, how hard is it for us to roll over to their side of the bed once in a while? Perhaps tonight is the night to bring it to him.

Making love is one of the best ways to express love to our husbands. Hundreds of cute notes or special dinners can't take the place of sex. Set a romantic mood one night this week and show your husband how much you love him physically. If you need to, pray for a better sex life. Pray that the Lord will give you the discipline to be there for your husband physically. Ask Him to help you find joy in the moment and the courage to be obedient to God's Word. Our Father in Heaven wants what is best for you and your marriage. A passionate sex life is worth going after as there is nothing that will draw you closer to your soul mate than making love.

Challenge

Make a move on your man this week. Whether it's showing up naked in bed or simply deciding to make that first move towards intimacy, just do it! If this is not a challenge for you because you are blessed with a wonderful sex life—do it anyway and reflect on how fortunate you are to have that gift.

Thirteen

But, Lord!

"Take away the stone." [Jesus] said. "But, Lord," said Martha, the sister of the dead man, "by this time there is a bad odor, for he has been there four days."

-John 11:39 NIV

Oxymoron. That figure of speech we learned about in high school combining two contradictory terms: jumbo shrimp, Loners Club, liquid gas, larger half, deafening silence or pretty ugly to name a few. Two words that just don't seem to belong together. Martha verbalized the ultimate oxymoron when she spoke to Jesus one afternoon about two thousand years ago—two little words that are black and white in contradiction: "But, Lord." Now that's an oxymoron. Saying *but* to our Lord is a definite opposition in terms. If He is truly our Lord, our response to Him, no matter what He requests, should be, "Yes, Lord."

Remember, a key ingredient in our Chocolate Cake Marriage is obedience to our Master Chef. If we call Jesus our Lord, then we should submit to Him and treat Him as Lord. Be obedient to His call. Heed His direction. Remember,

He has all the answers and is the Way, the Truth, and the Life. If we believe He is the Alpha and the Omega—omniscient, omnipotent, and omnipresent—why would we respond to His direction with, "But Lord?" Well, if we are honest, our answer might be, "Because we're human."

Yes, we are mere mortals. And it can be really, really hard to obey what God calls us to do at times, especially in our marriages. We want the Chocolate Cake Marriage. But, when our emotions are high, and the world is on our last nerve, we might hear a little voice whisper, "It's not worth the effort." Simply by definition, a marriage is a union of not only two sinners, but two sinners who are wired differently, with different interests, emotions, views, personalities ... and the list goes on. How can I press on and do what God calls me to do when that voice tells me to throw in the towel and do what I want?

Let's remember the nature of God. We know from His Word that our Heavenly Father is always looking out for our good. He seeks out ways to bless us. Desires to fill our lives with joy and peace. Uses all things for our good. He even tells us that discipline will bear a harvest of fruit. With those concepts in mind, anything He asks us to do would be for our benefit, right?

When God asks us to submit to and respect our husband, why are we so vulnerable to expressing the same words Martha did when God asked her to follow through on a simple request? Why have we all responded at one time or another to God's direction with Martha's same defiance when we stammer the challenge, "But, Lord?"

The scene is found in the eleventh chapter of the book of John, Lazarus, a dear friend of Jesus and the brother of Martha and Mary had fallen very ill. His sisters sent for Jesus to come quickly, but He told His disciples that He was not ready to go to them—that this was all happening so the Son of God would receive glory. So, Jesus remained where He was and did not heed the call to rush to the home of the desperate sisters. After a couple of days, Lazarus died, was wrapped in burial clothes, and placed in a tomb with the customary stone rolled in place to seal the grave.

Martha and Mary were mourning their brother, who had been buried for four days, when Jesus finally arrived. Mary threw herself at Jesus' feet crying out, "If only You had been here, my brother would not have died." Jesus asked to be taken to the tomb and once there, he told the crowd, "Take away the stone." It was then that the infamous oxymoron was voiced by Martha: "But, Lord, it has been four days since he died. There will be a bad smell."[64]

> *"Did I not tell you," replied Jesus, "that if you believed, you would see the wonder of what God can do?"*
> - John 11:40 PHILLIPS

Martha seemed to attempt to teach the Author of life about death and stench. Apparently, she felt the need to convey to the Lord of lords that there would be a really bad smell if they obeyed His order to take away the stone. Perhaps avoiding her own nasal distress, and focusing on her own aromatic comforts, Martha took God off the throne and questioned His instruction.

We get to witness Martha's humanity. She was hurting and not understanding why Jesus would let her dear brother die. Her pain was causing her to doubt His directive. Her sorrow and anguish lulled her into questioning Jesus' authority with a shadow of doubt. "But, Lord." My heart goes out to Martha because I, too, have let my own pain and anguish cause me to question God's instruction at times—or, even cause me to take a slight stance of rebellion.

"Doesn't God know that there will be a stench? Doesn't He know this is difficult?"

Jesus, the Creator of the Universe, the God Who placed the stars in the heavens, the One Who said, "Let there be light and there was light." He was the One Martha watched heal and perform miracles with her own eyes, and He asked her to take away a stone—a seemingly simple act. Yet she questioned Him and stated her argument—there will be a really bad smell. She was leery of His command. Skeptical of the Wonderful Counselor, Mighty God, Everlasting Father, Prince of Peace, Giver of life. Her response, "But, Lord," sounds so foolish in light of Whom she is speaking to—and yet, haven't we said the same thing so many times?

If God is the Lord of our lives and He calls us to do something, we need to trust the One who is communicating with us and ask the Holy Spirit to give us the strength to say, "*Yes*, Lord" instead of "*But*, Lord." When we say "Yes," we make way for the miracle. Not until *after* Jesus' command was obeyed—the stone ultimately rolled away—did everyone in attendance become privy to a miracle. A man who had been dead and decaying for four days walked out of the tomb and shed his grave clothes.

When "But, Lord" turned to "Yes, Lord," a man wrapped like a mummy from head to toe stepped out of a grave with a smile on his face and a spring in his step. A family leapt with joy at the wonder before their eyes. The glory of God was revealed. No stench! No decay! Just life and wonder. A heart beating and blood flowing. As a result of taking away the stone, pushing aside the "But, Lords" and obeying God, a miracle happens.

What happens if the stone is left in place? The crowd misses the miracle. The mourning remains. The tears of grief flow. The bitterness over death is left unchecked. A man is left in a tomb with stench and decay. Obedience set the miracle in motion. Heartache turned into happiness. Sorrow into savor. Mourning into marvel. Once Martha set her excuses and worldly logic aside, and the stone was rolled away, the miracle took place.

Martha's rationalization for not wanting to roll away the stone looks quite silly in hindsight. She almost missed the resurrection of her beloved brother because of the potential for a bad smell. She almost missed a miracle simply because she wasn't willing to trust God with the directive to roll away the stone. Martha simply needed to trust her Lord—as do we.

> *Obedience set the miracle in motion.*

Does your marriage need resurrecting? Does a healing need to take place? Perhaps, like Martha, you've been calling for Jesus. You have begged Him to come quickly because your marriage is sick and dying, but Jesus seems slow in coming. Doesn't He care? Will He even come at all? Then, when He finally arrived, it seemed too late—the marriage was already in the tomb, lifeless and wrapped in grave clothes. Yet when Jesus showed Himself, He decided not to answer your prayer to heal your marriage instantly. Instead, He asked something of you. He suggested you "take away the stone." However, like Martha, your response has been, "But, Lord. The smell will be really bad." You feel the need to explain to God that what He's asking you to do won't solve anything but will bring about a terrible stench.

Don't miss the resurrection, sweet sister. Simply trust and obey. Let go and let God. He is in the business of miracles, and He wants to perform one in your marriage. Don't focus on what He's asking you do, focus on the One who is all-powerful and all-knowing. Follow the command of the One who simply says, "Take away the stone," and then enjoy the front row seat of the miracle.

What stone is He asking you to take away? Maybe it is your lack of submission to your husband. However, are you quick to utter the oxymoron, *"But Lord, he's not a Christian"*? Or, *"But Lord, he will make bad decisions."* Or, *"But Lord, he's not good with our finances—we'll end up not making ends meet. If I submit to him, there will be a terrible stench!"*

Wives, it should be no different with your husbands.

Submit to them as you do to the Lord...

-Ephesians 5:22 VOICE

Don't make excuses like Martha did. Submit to your husband as to the Lord, and watch God do the miracle. He is our Immanuel—God with us—and He is with us to help us obey.

Does your stone have *Respect* etched on the top? God instructs wives explicitly to respect their husbands. He doesn't include any fine print clause that releases us from this one. To obey this command takes some serious dying to self. God's Word says, *"However, each man among you [without exception] is to love his wife as his very own self [with behavior worthy of respect and esteem, always seeking the best for her with an attitude of lovingkindness], and the wife [must see to it] that she respects and delights in her husband [that she notices him and prefers him and treats him with loving concern, treasuring him, honoring him, and holding him dear.]"*[65] This is a high calling for both spouses—let's ask God to enable us to adhere to our portion of the command.

Don't miss the miracle. Take away the stone.

Or perhaps God is asking you to make love more often with your husband, and your excuse has been, "But Lord, I just don't want to," or "I'm not in the mood," or "He doesn't do it right," or "We are on opposite schedules," or "I was abused as a child," or, or, or, or ...

Do not deprive each other of sexual relations, unless you both agree to refrain from sexual intimacy for a limited time so you can give yourselves more completely to prayer. Afterward, you should come together again so that Satan won't be able to tempt you because of your lack of self-control.

- 1 Corinthians 7:5

Take away the stone.

Has God been nudging you to quit nagging? Have you become your husband's substitute Holy Spirit? Getting on him about his faults, flaws and blunders? "But Lord, if I don't remind him about these things, he'll constantly overeat, overspend, overindulge, over-everything!"

Better to live alone in a tumbledown shack than
share a mansion with a nagging spouse.
- Proverbs 21:9 & 25:24 MSG

Here is another instance where God chose to put the same verse in His Word twice. He knew we required a reminder.

A nagging spouse is like the drip, drip, drip of a leaky faucet;

you can't turn it off, and you can't get away from it.

- Proverbs 27:15 MSG

Take away the stone.

Do you need to roll away the hours spent on social media or binge watching? Time thieves include: Facebook, Instagram, Snapchat, emailing, surfing the web, Netflix, Hulu, and the list does go on. Oh, how easy it is to spend a couple of hours lounging in front of the TV or perusing Instagram, then claim we don't have the time to do Bible study or go for a walk. "But Lord, I need my down time."

Plus, they get into the habit of being idle. Not only are they idle, but

they band together and roam from house to house, gossiping about and

meddling into other people's business; they talk about all

sorts of things that should never be spoken of.

- 1 Timothy 5:13 VOICE

Perhaps rather than going from house to house, we are going from page to page on Facebook, or Instagram. Social media has become a place where "they talk about all sorts of things that should never be spoken of."

Take away the stone.

Are you involved in friendships or relationships that pull you down or influence you in ungodly ways? Maybe you're joining other wives for husband-bashing sessions and getting ungodly marital advice. "But Lord, they are my friends, I need someone to vent with."

> *Do not be deceived: Bad company corrupts good morals.*
> *- 1 Corinthians 15:33 AMP*

Take away the stone.

Is your boulder sipping too much wine, smoking pot, taking prescription drugs, or using other narcotics? Do Friday Night parties with friends cause you to stumble and allow alcohol or drugs to influence your behavior and consequently your marriage? "But Lord, everyone else is. It's only a few glasses, or a joint once in a while. I'm an adult. It's legal."

> *Too much wine begins to mock you,*
> *too much strong drink leads to noisy fights,*
> *and whoever is misled by either is not wise.*
> *- Proverbs 20:1 VOICE*

> *Don't drink too much wine. That cheapens your life.*
> *Drink the Spirit of God, huge draughts of him.*
> *- Ephesians 5:18 MSG*

Take away the stone.

Could gossip or hanging out with those who do be the stone blocking your miracle? Oh, this habit so easily trickles into our lives and gets in the way of God's blessings. His Word says that He will not answer prayers when we habitually choose to sin.[66] Let's get serious about allowing God's Word to be a lamp to our feet so we can be examples to those around us.

A gossip betrays a confidence;

so avoid anyone who talks too much.

- Proverbs 20:19 NIV

Wrongdoers perk up when listening to gossip,

and liars lean in close to hear talk of mischief.

- Proverbs 17:4 VOICE

Your persistent wrong doing has come between you and your God;

since you constantly reject and push God away,

He had to turn aside and ignore your cries.

- Isaiah 59:2 VOICE

Take away the stone.

Perhaps a hobby simply takes too much of your time. Hobbies can be wonderful—even ministry minded. However, if we are spending five hours a day scrapbooking or creating Instagram posts while our house is a mess, laundry's not done, and the only thing for dinner is what's in the freezer, then we have a stone to move. "But, Lord, my hobby helps me escape. It keeps me sane."

She directs the activities of her household,

and never does she indulge in laziness.

- Proverbs 31:27 VOICE

Take away the stone.

Has the Lord asked you to forgive your husband—perhaps for something really hard for you to forgive and forget? God is standing before the tomb asking you to take away the stone of unforgiveness. So far, all you've been able to muster up is a hushed whisper, "But Lord, he hurt me so badly. What if he does it again? He needs to pay for what he did. I can't forgive him."

> *God is standing before the tomb asking you to take away the stone of unforgiveness.*

If you forgive those who sin against you, your heavenly

Father will forgive you. But if you refuse to forgive

others, your Father will not forgive your sins.

- Matthew 6:14-15

Make allowance for each other's faults and forgive anyone

who offends you. Remember, the Lord

forgave you, so you must forgive others.

- Colossians 3:13

Take away the stone.

What simple act occurred in order to see the miraculous resurrection of

Lazarus? A stone was removed. Obedience was put into action. Excuses were set aside. Doubt was conquered. *"But, Lords"* became *"Yes, Lords."* In the face of skepticism, a stone was rolled away. What was once dead is alive! Are you looking for a miracle in your marriage? Ask Jesus what needs to be rolled away.

Despite Martha's doubts, when the stone was finally moved from Lazarus' tomb, there wasn't a stench—there was the aroma of life. There wasn't putrefaction, but purification. Not a rotting corpse, but a restored spirit. Death became life. Don't let what you *think* will happen when you remove the stone get in the way of your obedience to God's call to roll it away. Leave the outcome to Him. He says if you love Me, you will obey what I command. Anticipate the miracle. He will bring about the resurrection; you just need to provide the obedience. It will give a whole new meaning to rolling stones!

How do we go beyond believing *in* God, to actually believing Him and His promises? What will it take to set aside the doubt and defiance necessary in order to have the strength to roll away our stone? When we decide to trust and obey Him, what's next? How do we dislodge that big boulder that stands between us and a resurrected marriage? If we don't feel strong enough to budge it, we only have to look to the God who stands with us. Our God moves mountains.

> *"I tell you the truth, if you had faith even as small as a mustard seed, you*
> *could say to this mountain, 'Move from here to there,' and it would move.*
> *Nothing would be impossible.*
> - Matthew 17:20b

God will bless obedience. The stone in front of Lazarus' tomb was tiny compared to the size of a mountain, yet God says with the faith of a teeny-tiny mustard seed, we can move mountains. Imagine what we can do to stones! We can flick those with our little finger—like flicking an ant off our picnic table. We simply have to submit to God's authority and do what He asks.

God can do anything you know—far more than you could ever imagine or guess or request in your wildest dreams! He does it not by pushing us around but by working within us, his Spirit deeply and gently within us.

- Ephesians 3:20-21 MSG

Challenge

Find a stone. Pick one up from your backyard, while on a walk in the park, or from the local nursery. Your rock can be shiny and pretty, or rugged and dirty— it's your stone. Set it somewhere you will see it daily to remind you of the stone you plan to take away. Ask the Lord to show you where you have called out, "But, Lord," and then choose to say, "Yes, Lord." Perhaps look to the list on the previous pages to help you determine what stone needs to be rolled away from your tomb. Then, "Do it!" Don't miss out on the resurrection any longer. A man waits to come out with new life breathed into him and wants to rip off his grave clothes—perhaps that man is your husband.

Fourteen

Is There Something in My Eye?

Why is it that you see the dust in your brother's or sister's eye,
but you can't see what is in your own eye?

Matthew 7:3 VOICE

"Happy wife, happy life." There's some truth spoken in these four words. What about "peaceful spouse, peaceful house?" Typically, if husbands and wives are at peace with each other, happiness ensues. To access harmony, we need to determine to step out in faith to make changes—even if we seem to be the only one doing the altering. The byproduct will be change in our husbands too. Seek God's instruction and obey Him when He gives guidance on how to be a godly wife. So often our husbands are not the men we want them to be because we aren't the wives God has called us to be. Ouch. I know that's not easy to hear, but you made it this far, so you are up for the challenge, right?

If we continue to point fingers—aiming our manicured digit at our husbands, stating they are to blame for all the marriage difficulties—what good will

Does the blame game have any winners?

that do? Does the blame game have any winners? Will our husbands change because we present mountains of evidence that they need to? Usually not. Even if our husbands are partly to blame for the strife, it takes two to tango. When we point a finger at someone else, we have three fingers pointed back at ourselves—I know because I was an expert at finger pointing.

God has much to say about taming our own behavior before we seek changes in our men. Yes, our husbands need tune-ups, but as I stated earlier, don't make the mistake of trying to be your husband's Holy Spirit. God truly does not need our help convicting our husbands of their sin. God needs you and me to be obedient to our own convictions. God holds up a mirror and asks us to search our own hearts and then begin our own alteration process.

> *"Why do you look at the speck of sawdust in your brother's eye and*
> *pay no attention to the plank in your own eye?"*
> - Luke 6:41 NIV

I love candles and often have multiple wicks lit throughout our home. One evening, my husband counted forty-seven flickering flames as guests were due to arrive! Jar candles and little votives in pretty glass holders are my favorite. The glow of the dancing flames and the lovely fragrance provide a sweet ambiance and put me in a peaceful frame of mind. I am drawn to candles and enjoy how they illuminate a room with soft light. That kind of radiance reminds me of the light God has called us to be.

You are like that illuminating light. Let your light shine everywhere you go, that you may illumine creation, so men and women everywhere may see

your good actions, may see creation at its fullest, may see your devotion to

Me, and may turn and praise your Father in heaven because of it.

- Matthew 5:16 VOICE

I think it is important to consider what kind of light we produce as our husband's wife and helpmate. Are we comparable to the flickering candle flame with a sweet aroma? Is our fragrance delicate—one that draws our husbands to us, and ultimately to our Savior? Or maybe we reflect the glow of a warm, crackling fire that invites our spouse to join us in the warmth and peacefulness we radiate.

Keep in mind, not all forms of illumination are pleasing. Let's check to make sure we are not giving off the wrong light.

Satan himself poses as a messenger of heavenly light.

- 2 Corinthians 11:14 VOICE

In the early years of my first marriage, rather than the flickering glow of an aromatic candle, my light source became more like a blowtorch—a harsh, loud, intense blaze. The kind of light that would make any husband reach for a protective faceguard, back away and avoid the burning fire. Faultfinding, finger pointing, and blaming were kindling. Oh, I shudder to think how many times I "burned" him with that kind of light. I needed a warning sticker on my torch: *Caution, contents may be flammable and prone to explosion.* This was not the kind of light Jesus had in mind when He told us to be the salt and light of the earth.[67] My intentions were good, but my method needed to be extinguished. I truly wanted to have a home where God was honored, and our boys could be led down the path of godliness. However, my tactics were often glaring and left a few too many first-degree burns. God wants us to be an example of His light, and He will enable us to do that if we will seek Him to be our source of radiance.

> *For if your whole body is full of light, with no part of it in shadow, it will all be radiant—it will be like having a bright lamp to give you light."*
>
> - Luke 11:36 Phillips

What kind of light are we emitting? Is it a blinding spotlight shining harshly into the eyes of our mates? The kind of light police officers use during a "Where were you on December 7th at four o'clock" interrogation? Inquiring and condemning. Resisting our husbands rather than drawing them in for constructive communication? Do our husbands enjoy our company? They are the ones that we should show the most kindness and consideration to, more than anyone else in the entire world, because we made a covenant with them, and no one else. Are they seeing that in us? Would you want to come home each night to you? It's a fair question to ask.

If we could watch a video replay of how we interact with our men, the ones we made vows to love, honor and cherish, would we like what we see? If we become someone our husbands don't want to spend time with, they might look for reasons to stay away from constant critique and agitation. Be a light who draws your husband in, not one who repels him. Let's determine to reflect the light of Christ. The moon darkens and disappears when it does not reflect the sun, and we too become dimly lit when we do not reflect the Son.

Ultimately, we want to attract our husbands, not continually confront them with their faults and failures. To avoid the heat of the torch, our husbands might begin to put in more hours at the office or play a few more rounds of golf. Maybe they'll try to tune us out by watching more television or surfing the net. Whatever the outlet, they will find a way to avoid the clashes and critiques. Let's be wives who entice our husbands.

I find it interesting that the origin of the word *entice* most likely comes from an old French word with the base meaning of "set on fire." Be on fire for Jesus and shine a dramatic light that sparkles like a 200-carat diamond—entice your husband, sweet sister. Nobody likes to be around someone who is harsh and critical all the time. In fact, we all naturally shy away from people like that.

If your husband has areas that need correcting, let God bring the conviction when change is needed. The Holy Spirit will shine a spotlight onto the areas your husband needs to work on so much better than we ever could. We simply need to reflect Jesus, be on our knees in prayer, let go and let God!

> *You should clothe yourselves instead with the beauty that comes from*
> *within, the unfading beauty of a gentle and quiet spirit,*
> *which is so precious to God.*
>
> - 1 Peter 3:4

Meditate on that verse for a moment. Ask yourself, "Do I reflect a gentle and quiet spirit? Does my reputation inside the four walls of my own home register a ten for harshness or a ten for gentleness?" If this is an area you need to work on, don't beat yourself up. If you scored a little higher on the harshness meter, take it to the Lord. Ask Him to mold you into a quieter, gentler version of

Do I reflect a gentle and quiet spirit?

yourself, and He will transform your heart. One of the fruits of the Spirit is gentleness, so ask God to blend that into your character supernaturally. Pray before you speak and use spiritual duct tape a little more often. Take James's advice:

> *Let everyone be quick to hear [be a careful, thoughtful listener], slow to*
> *speak [a speaker of carefully chosen words and],*
> *slow to anger [patient, reflective, forgiving]*
> *- James 1:19b AMP*

God wants to work gentleness into your character—allow Him to do it by obeying His instructions.

Wives often become masters at pointing out the faults in their husbands, forgetting God's detailed instructions regarding fault-finding. The Lord calls us to first take a look at our own flaws and adjust our own behaviors to remove those iniquities from our own lives—allowing the Holy Spirit to do a work in our heart first. Then, and only then, can we even consider pointing out the speck in our husband's eye.[68]

Many husbands love sports and have been known to take in their fair share of television. Perhaps your man loves his recliner and can channel-surf like he's riding a Hawaiian wave. We may see the big screen in our living room as the "other woman." After all, our husband might spend countless hours with her, gazing into her eyes, and pushing all her buttons. When our husband settles in to view a show, are we primed and ready to deliver the *"You are such a couch potato"* speech?

This dialog tends to be delivered with hand on hip and voice raised a notch. We want our men to fit into our mold of "perfect husband," which does not leave room for idleness in front of the television for any length of time. There are things to do around here! Somehow, in that moment, our memory does not call to mind all the things our husbands have already taken care of that week. We tend to think, if I don't get to sit around and watch TV at this very moment, then why does he?

Don't be a Nagging Nancy, sweet sister. I believe God wants us to be good stewards of our time, and we all know television can be a time-vampire. However, we need to obey the command *thou shalt not nag* and let God nudge our husbands to use their time wisely. And perhaps before we try to dig the splinter out of his eye, we consider removing the log from our own eye first. Maybe, just maybe.

Webster's defines nag: *to find fault incessantly: complain.*[69] Are we incessantly finding fault with our husbands? Even with the best of intentions? We are disobeying God's word when we nag, which means nagging is a sin. Sin separates us from God, so if this is an area you struggle with, stop nagging today. It can be that simple. Repent and ask God's Spirit to help you break the habit.

God continues His admonition against nagging by telling us that our husbands would be better off on the corner of a roof than to live with a nag. Go ahead, get a picture in your mind of your husband hunched over on the roof of your home, surrounded by dust and pigeon poop, balanced precariously on the corner, with a slight wind blowing. God is saying he is better off up there than with us if we are nagging wives. A good reason to stop nagging.

The origin of the word *nag* is interesting—in the original dialect, *nag* actually meant *gnaw*. You know, like a dog gnaws on a bone. Can you picture us gnawing our husbands to death by nagging? Such a sad, unpleasant picture. Yet, that is what we do if we allow ourselves to fall into this habit. We are all prone to it, but we are never *within our rights* to go against God's Word. We can't justify nagging by saying "Otherwise, he won't get anything done." If you are constantly prodding your husband to do something, or not to do something, you are nagging.

What should we do if we ask our husbands to do something for us, and they just don't get it done? There are a few options. We can just let it go. Is it imperative that the task gets done? Or is it just that it will make us happy if it's done? One year, I really wanted my husband to get a huge box of photos out of a storage unit, but it did not make it onto his top 20 list of things to get done. He had so much going on in his life at that time that I realized I needed to let it go. Not everything we want needs to happen.

Another option is to do the task ourselves. If we choose this route, we need to make sure we don't take care of the issue with an attitude of, "Fine, I'll just do it myself." Giving our husband a chance to complete the chore is an important form of respect. Ultimately, the main point is to pray about the issue and wait for God to lead and guide. God really does care about the little things in our lives.[70]

The cousin to Nagging Nancy is Quarrelsome Quinn. If you are constantly bickering, you are a quarrelsome wife.

> *A quarrelsome wife is like the dripping of a leaky roof in a rainstorm...*
> - Proverbs 27:15 NIV

No matter how much we sugarcoat our nagging and quarreling as "just trying to get things done around the house," if our actions come in the form of a constant dripping, we need to turn off the faucet.

Let's get in line with God's desires for us as wives, and let the Holy Spirit do the convicting of our husbands' habits, if that is indeed God's plan. We have to trust God and follow His lead—we just might end up seeing a few miracles.

There are times when I want to wag my finger at my husband for watching TV, but I can conveniently forget the times that I have spent a few hours in front of the black box. After a long day, I can easily flop in front of the television to watch *America's Got Talent* or the late-breaking news just to turn off my brain for a while. Who was I to give my husband a *hand on hip* speech about TV viewing habits? I need to remember to yank the plank out of my own eye before reaching for the tweezers to pick the speck out of my husband's. Once again, God's Word provides the simple instruction:

> *That type of criticism and judgment is a sham! Remove the plank from your own eye, and then perhaps you will be able to see clearly how to help your brother flush out his sawdust.*
>
> - Matthew 7:5 VOICE

Just because I was choosing to watch television at different times than my husband, did not make the time less wasted. When I stayed up too late to finish watching a movie, it's just as much a time-robber, not to mention sleep-stealer, as my husband watching the post-game show. I needed to get my TV habits in check before I have any business trying to influence my husband's viewing practices. Otherwise, God dubs me a hypocrite. Ouch!

Notice that God encourages us to get the plank out of our eye *in order* to be able to see clearly to flush the sawdust out of our brother's eye. It's not that we are banned from pointing out specks—there are behaviors that might need soul-searching and altering. We are simply called to examine our own behaviors first, and then go, in love, to encourage others to be the best they can be in God's eyes.

So, practically speaking, if there is a situation in your marriage that needs discussion, first pray about it. Ask the Lord for His timing and for His words. You may find after praying about it, that the subject is not something the Lord wants *you* to discuss with your man. Perhaps God has someone else in mind to go speck-plucking. If so, you will have avoided potential strife and discord between you and your spouse. If God brings someone else to man the tweezers, praise Him for it.

However, if a circumstance warrants communication, and God is calling you to be the spokesperson, talk to your husband in love. Pray for the Lord to orchestrate the timing and to give your husband listening ears and the desire to model the heart of Christ. Ask the Holy Spirit to guide you when you speak, and to assist your husband with the listening—even if he is not a believer.

> *But the Advocate, the Holy Spirit, whom the Father will send in my name, will teach you all things and will remind you of everything I have said to you.*
> - John 14:26 NIV

If you wait on the Lord's direction, He will give you the timing and the words. Then, let go and let God. As an added bonus, when we speak to our men God's way, we have a far greater chance of them hearing us because nagging usually ends up falling on deaf ears anyway.

I'd like to suggest one other thought to ponder. Often what we dislike the most about someone else's mannerisms or behaviors is what we dis-like about our *own* actions. Does our husband's irritating habit hold up a mirror to our own conduct? Is that why the behavior bothers us so much? Perhaps it irritates us when he answers his phone during our dinner date, but we answer our phone when at lunch with friends. Be aware that the irritating habit our husbands have might be something we are guilty of ourselves, in a slightly different way.

I encourage you to reflect on that, and if there is an area or activity that the Lord wants to work out of you first, get out the ax and chop up that plank. Throw the two-by-four into the wood chipper. Let's be obedient to what God teaches us before we examine and critique others. James says,

> *Don't fool yourself into thinking that you are a listener when you are anything but, letting the Word go in one ear and out the other. Act on what you hear! Those who hear and don't act are like those who glance in the mirror, walk away, and two minutes later have no idea who they are, what they look like.*
> - James 1:22-24 MSG

Challenge

Have you been nagging your husband about one of his habits? Perhaps he drives too fast, chews too loudly, or leaves his towel on the floor. Write it down on a 3x5 card and commit it to prayer. Decide today that you will obey God's instruction to be a praying wife, not a nagging wife. Stop bringing the behavior to your husband's attention—he lives it, he knows about it. Get on your knees, ask God to help him overcome it, and see what the Lord will do as you obey His instructions.

> *Love bears all things [regardless of what comes], believes all things [looking for the best in each one], hopes all things [remaining steadfast during difficult times], endures all things [without weakening].*
>
> - 1 Corinthians 13:7 AMP

Fifteen

Bringing Sparkle Back

On that day the Lord their God will rescue his people, just as a shepherd rescues his sheep. They will sparkle in his land like jewels in a crown.

- Zechariah 9:16

The final ingredient to blend into your Chocolate Cake Marriage is joy. Even when the circumstances behind our four walls seem dull, dark and depressing, or when the pressures and concerns, worries and trials weigh us down, we need God's sparkle of light that accompanies gladness.

Daniel tells us:

Those who are wise will shine as bright as the sky, and those who lead many to righteousness will shine like the stars forever.

- Daniel 12:3

The Message translation puts it this way:

Men and women who have lived wisely and well will shine brilliantly, like the cloudless, star-strewn night skies. And those who put others on the

right path to life will glow like stars forever.

- Daniel 12:3 MSG

Webster's Dictionary defines *sparkle*:[71]

to give off or reflect bright moving points of light

to cause to shine

to perform very well

to become lively or animated

These are all things we want to do as women. We want to reflect light. We want to cause others to shine. We want to perform well. And we want to become bright and lively. But how can we do this practically when sometimes it's a struggle to even smile at our neighbor?

Diamonds are the toughest substance on earth, yet even they can lose their sparkle if they are not handled with care. The daily wear and tear of life can erase the sparkle from a beautiful diamond ring. The same is true for a daughter of the King—the wear and tear of life can dull our shine, but we can take steps towards maintaining our sparkle.

When looking at a diamond under a microscope, we can see the build-up of tiny substances that diminish the sparkle from the precious stone. As women determined to follow God's recipe, we want to maintain our sparkle so nothing can cover the glistening, bright points of light.

Jesus tells us:

"I am the light of the world. If you follow me, you won't have to walk in darkness, because you will have the light that leads to life."

- John 8:12

He floods the darkness with light...

- Job 12:22a TLB

Perhaps you feel a shadow of darkness in your world. You need a little "diamond cleaner" to bring back that sparkle. Take your requests to God and let Him polish you up.

Romans 12:11-12 (MSG) tells us:

Don't burn out; keep yourselves fueled and aflame. Be alert servants of the Master, cheerfully expectant. Don't quit in hard times; pray all the harder.

Don't burn out because your marriage is hard—maintain your sparkle. The whole point of a trial is to change us—to make us more like Jesus so we can show a dark world there is a Savior ready to light up our lives. Jesus tells us to be that light to that world.

And you, beloved, are the light of the world. A city built on a hilltop cannot be hidden.

- Matthew 5:14 VOICE

Read Matthew 5:14-15 in the Message translation:

"Here's another way to put it: You're here to be light, bringing out the God-colors in the world. God is not a secret to be kept. We're going public with this, as public as a city on a hill. If I make you light-bearers, you don't think I'm going to hide you under a bucket, do you? I'm putting you on a light stand. Now that I've put you there on a hilltop, on a light stand—shine!"

One of the most beautiful ways we can honor God is to give off sparkly bling-bling light when we are going through a trial. Difficulties in our marriage can be a striking backdrop to display God's glory. God wants us to shine for Him so that the world will ask, "Who is this God that gives her hope and light even in the midst of a dark valley?"

Billy Graham's daughter, Anne Graham Lotz, wrote this beautiful devotion that depicts how we can shine in our trials:

Jesus Revealed in Us

Those who suffer according to God's will should commit themselves to their faithful Creator and continue to do good. - 1 Peter 4:19 NIV

If our kids always behave
and our boss is always pleased
and our home is always orderly
and our bodies always feel good

and we are patient and kind and thoughtful and happy and loving, others

shrug because they're capable of being that way too.

On the other hand, if we have a splitting headache,

the kids are screaming,

the phone is ringing,

the supper is burning,

yet we are still patient, kind, thoughtful, happy, and loving, the world sits

up and takes notice. The world knows that kind of behavior is not natural.

It's supernatural.

And others see Jesus revealed in us.[72]

Of course, we want to shine when things are going well too, but people tend to be more curious about the source of light shining out of utter darkness.

A key element of my sparkle maintenance is a daily quiet time with the Lord. Sitting with Him. Opening up my Bible to hear from Him. Praying to Him. Enjoying an intimate relationship with my Savior.

Having a bond with someone takes time and effort. If you stop spending time with a friend and resort to only an occasional text or Facebook message, soon your friendship will fade, and you won't even recognize her voice on the other end of a phone call. You will not have the depth and joy your relationship had when it was based on time spent together and shared experiences.

Always ready and available to spend time with us, Jesus desires a close intimate relationship with His kids. We are the ones who walk away and miss out on the sweetness of a relationship based on abiding in Him. Let's determine to keep our friendship with Jesus fresh. As you walk through changes and challenges in your marriage, trust in God to get you through any trials with peace, strength, and yes, sparkle!

Remember this ingredient from God's recipe.

People with their minds set on you, you keep completely whole,
Steady on their feet, because they keep at it and don't quit.
- Isaiah 26:3 MSG

The NIV translation puts it this way:

You will keep in perfect peace those whose minds are steadfast,
because they trust in you.
- Isaiah 26:3 NIV

If we want peace, we need steadfast minds. What does steadfast mean, exactly? Turning again to Webster's Dictionary, we learn the meaning is: Firmly fixed in place; firm in belief, determination, or adherence.[73] We need our eyes firmly fixed on Jesus in order to respond the way He wants us to when facing trials.

God has a plan. The Alpha and Omega will get us from A to Z. We just need to trust Him when He gives us direction. He wants to use the difficulties we face for good, and ultimately for His glory.

In Jeremiah Chapter 33, an entire chapter about God's promised restoration, God says:

> *Call to me and I will answer you. I'll tell you marvelous and won-*
> *drous things that you could never figure out on your own*
> - Jeremiah 33:3 MSG

Do you believe God is sovereign? Do you trust that He has allowed whatever is going on in your life right now? Do you believe He will work out all things for good for you because you love Him and have been called according to His purpose?

Choose to follow His recipe, sweet sister and He will use you to reflect light from the Son.

We are reminded in God's Word that He does allow bad things to happen.

> *Matters not who says a thing will or won't happen unless the Lord*
> *determines that it should. Most High God must proclaim it so*
> *—for both good and bad, joy and sorrow come from Him ...*
> - Lamentations 3:37-38 VOICE

Through the Holy Spirit, we don't need to simply endure trials; we can also reveal to others where we get our strength and peace. If we are no different than the world during a trial, then what will produce the curiosity to know Jesus? Our marriages can be the tools the Lord uses to draw onlookers peering into your world to seek our Savior.

> *And you, beloved, are the light of the world. A city built on a*
> *hilltop cannot be hidden. Similarly, it would be silly to light a*
> *lamp and then hide it under a bowl. When someone lights a lamp,*
> *she puts it on a table or a desk or a chair, and the light illumines*
> *the entire house. You are like that illuminating light.*
> *Let your light shine everywhere you go,*
> *that you may illumine creation, so men and women*
> *everywhere may see your good actions,*
> *may see creation at its fullest, may see your devotion to Me,*
> *and may turn and praise your Father in heaven because of it.*
> *- Matthew 5:14-16 VOICE*

Are you ready to reflect God's light today? Do you trust He will use all things for good? We get to be used by God when we let our light shine everywhere we go. Trust your marriage and all the trials you go through to the One who placed the stars in the heavens and the breath in your lungs.

If we settle for an ordinary relationship with God, we cannot expect to have an extraordinary relationship with our husbands. Get to know your God, and He will transform you and your marriage. Then, you will be that light on the hill shining His love and peace to the world, and to your husband.

The wonderful truth about reflecting light is that we don't have to muster up the power to reflect. We don't need to find some way to make ourselves shine—that would be exhausting. We simply need to hang out with God—He will bathe us in light, and we will glow.

God is God, he has bathed us in light.

- Psalm 118:27 MSG

Just like how the moon reflects the sun and lights up the entire sky on a cool winter's night, we can reflect the Son and light up the world.

Commit your way to the Lord; trust in him and he will do this: He will make your righteous reward shine like the dawn, your vindication like the noonday sun. Be still before the Lord and wait patiently for him;

- Psalm 37:5-7 NIV

A diamond shines the brightest when it reflects light, especially the powerful light of the sun. As daughters of the King, we shine our brightest when we reflect the Son, Jesus Christ. Commit your way to Him, and you will shine your brightest.

When a jeweler presents a diamond to a potential buyer, he typically places the precious stone on black velvet because light sparkles brightest against a dark backdrop. This is true in our lives as well. God will allow us to go through dark, painful valleys as the Master Jeweler presents our lives against a backdrop where He knows we will shine the brightest.

He is I AM. Yahweh. He is the infinite, all-knowing, mighty God who created the Universe. Trust Him. Remember Daniel 12:3 (MSG):

Men and women who have lived wisely and well will shine brilliantly, like the cloudless, star-strewn night skies. And those who put others on the right path to life will glow like stars forever.

\- Daniel 12:3 MSG

As we journey through any valley during our time on earth, let's help to lead as many as we can to righteousness, and we will glow like a star forever. Otherwise, we might be wasting the trial that God wants to use to bring others to Him. My walk with the Lord is so much deeper because of trials I have been through, many of these were marriage-related. I am not amazing because I got through numerous trials with peace, strength and a sparkle. God is amazing because He gave His incredible peace and strength to a mere mortal, a cracked pot, and a flawed woman. He allowed me to shine on the darkest nights. Will you let Him use you and your marriage to reflect His light? You will be blessed for your obedience.

I hope this poem the Lord gave me will encourage you to be a light bearer for Jesus.

Bringing Sparkle Back

by Michelle Sullivan

Our life should be a vessel used to shine forth our Savior's light,

Will you offer your life to Him right now; choose to walk by faith not sight?

Like the moon reflects the sun which gives off that lunar glow,

Choose to reflect the Father's Son so that the world will know.

That though we are far from perfect, and make mistakes along the way,

God is doing a work, making changes day by day.

His Holy Spirit dwells within, wanting to correct and lead and guide,

We simply need to obey and trust, in Him we must abide.

God tells us to share His love with every tongue and tribe and nation,

We are called to be the salt and light to the entire population.

But if we have lost our saltiness, how will we cause them to thirst?

And if they don't thirst and turn to Him, their eternal fate is cursed.

Let's decide today to be that salt and light—women with God's sparkle,

Spreading God's love wherever we go, hoping to share the gospel.

It takes strong determination to follow God's narrow trail,

Remember He will never leave you nor forsake you. His love will never fail.

God will always give you the strength you need; just determine to never quit.

Stay close to Him and in His Word, and your light will stay brightly lit.

The enemy does slither around looking for someone to devour,

But be that woman after God's own heart, and he'll slink away and cower.

God does allow things in our lives that test us and make us grow,

Keep trusting in Him and He'll lead you along and show you which way to go.

Even when bad news comes, and life seems to throw you a curve,

Or the strains and pressures of this world have everyone on your last nerve.

Determine to reflect God's Son in your every thought and deed,

Like providing a cup of water to an enemy in need.

This is how a dying world will notice we shine God's light,

When we offer love not hate, an act of kindness instead of a fight.

God tells us to turn from our own wicked ways so He can heal our land,

Let's start today to turn the other cheek and offer a helping hand.

Let's respect our husbands, love our kids and honor our fathers and mothers,

Follow God's lead and do what He says when we want to know how to treat others.

Stop the hiss of gossip, and the drinking of too much wine,

Don't have sex before marriage and stop all the arguing and lying.

End the swearing and cursing and using God's name in vain,

Instead, meditate on His Word, and pray in Jesus' Name.

This is how we win a lost world to know that God sent His only Son,

Who lived, and died and rose again, He is the Holy One.

We are called to be a beacon; to light the way to meet our amazing Lord,

Showing the world there is a reason that His precious blood was poured.

You might be surprised by who is peering into your own little world today,

To observe who is this Jesus that you have decided to obey.

Live each moment knowing that your life is making a mark,

It's all in choosing to do right not wrong, living a life that is set apart.

Don't beat yourself up if change is needed, we are all a work in progress,

He offers forgiveness at the foot of the cross, where His blood will give you access.

He'll give you the peace and strength, and help you become your very best,

He's taken your sins and cast them as far as the east is from the west!

We are daughters of the King of kings, and in Him there's nothing that we lack,

Let's make today the day that we start bringing Sparkle back!

We are the bride of Christ, dear one. Daughters of the King.

Never forget that powerful truth.

We know He gave Himself up completely to make her His own, washing her clean of all her impurity with water and the powerful presence of His word. He has given Himself so that He can present the church as His radiant bride, unstained, unwrinkled, and unblemished—completely free from all impurity—holy and innocent before Him.

- Ephesians 5:26-27 VOICE

The relationship between a husband and wife is used as the word picture to illustrate Christ's love for the church. Christ the bridegroom loves, adores, and sacrifices for His bride. In our brokenness, we will never measure up to that kind of unconditional, sacrificial love towards our spouses, but can we give it our best shot? Can we love our husbands even when it's difficult? Even when we don't feel loved and when everything in us is saying, "It's not worth it"?

When onlookers pull back the curtain and peek into our marriages, we have an opportunity to show them what Christ's love looks like. If strife, disrespect, and broken promises are all the world sees, what would make people want to know the Savior we claim to know?" I can only imagine what might happen if we got serious about loving and respecting our husbands, forgiving seven times seventy, not keeping record of wrongs, and modeling grace and mercy. The lost just might get curious about this carpenter from Nazareth. They just might choose to inquire more about our risen Savior who brings the dead to life. Choose to follow God's Word, dear one, and perhaps we'll see Chocolate Cake at Christ's glorious banquet—and there will be a few more people joining us around the table because we trusted His recipe.

. . . he answered their prayer because they trusted in Him.

- 1 Chronicles 5:20b

Michelle's Mud Pie

1 pkg. Oreo cookies

¾ cup Butter

½ cup Cocoa

¾ cup Sugar

1-quart Denali Extreme Maximum Fudge Moose Tracks Ice Cream

1-quart Mint Chocolate Chip Ice Cream

1-1/2 cups Heavy Whipping Cream

3 tsps. Vanilla Extract

Crush Oreo cookies in a large bowl into medium crumbs.

In a large saucepan, over medium heat, melt ½ cup of butter.

Stir in Oreo crumbs and coat crumbs with butter.

Press mixture into a 9" spring-form pan.

Bake at 375°F for 9 minutes.

Cool crust completely. [Pop in the freezer to speed up the cooling.]

Spread slightly softened Mint Chocolate Chip Ice Cream over crust. Then spread Extreme Moose Tracks Ice Cream to form second layer.

Freeze until firm [approximately 2 hours].

When pie is close to being firm, melt ¼ cup of butter in a medium saucepan over medium heat. Add cocoa, ½ cup sugar and ½ cup whipping cream stirring constantly.

When mixture is smooth and boils, remove from heat for 5 minutes.

Reheat mixture until it is bubbling again. Remove from heat.

Cool mixture slightly and add 2 tsps. Vanilla extract.

Pour over ice cream. Return pie to freezer and freeze for one hour.

In a small bowl, beat remaining whip cream, ¼ cup sugar and 1 tsp Vanilla extract until medium peaks form. Store whipped cream in refrigerator until it's time to serve mud pie.

When it's time, spread the whip cream on top of the mud pie and cut to serve.

Enjoy!

Notes

Endnotes

1	Joel 2:25
2	Matthew 19:26
3	Philippians 1:6
4	Genesis 6:22 *NIV*
5	Genesis 6:9
6	Jeremiah 29:11
7	Matthew 17:20
8	2 Chronicles 7:14
9	Romans 8:28 AMP
10	John 10:10
11	Psalm 103:12
12	John 3:16
13	Revelation 4:8
14	John 3:3
15	John 1:1
16	Psalm 103:12
17	Proverbs 22:6
18	Hebrews 13:5
19	Matthew 7:7a
20	Matthew 18:22
21	Psalm 46:10
22	Joel 2:25
23	Isaiah 61:3
24	Genesis 3:15a
25	Jeremiah 29:11
26	Isaiah 26:3
27	Philippians 4:13
28	Retrieved May 2018 from www2.bakersfieldcollege.edu/cfeer/Criminal%20Law/Text%20Pollock/chapter_9.ppt
29	Matthew 19:26
30	Retrieved in May 2018 from https://www.rainscourt.com/10-surprising-facts-divorce-uk/
31	Mark 10:9
32	Matthew 18:22
33	John 5:6
34	John 5:7-9 *NIV*
35	Romans 8:28
36	Isaiah 55:9
37	Mud Pie Recipe – see Appendix
38	Philippians 4:8
39	Colossians 3:23
40	Colossians 3:24
41	Genesis 3:1
42	Hebrews 11:25
43	Romans 6:16
44	Galatians 5:22-23
45	Ephesians 6:11
46	Ephesians 6:16,17
47	Philippians 1:6
48	Mark 10:8
49	Matthew 19:26
50	Eggerich, Emerson. *Love and Respect,* p. 32-33

51   2 Chronicles 7:14
52   respect. 2011. In *Merriam-Webster.com*.
        Retrieved April, 2018, from https://www.merriam-webster.com/dictionary/respect
53   Retrieved in May 2018 from *https://goodmenproject.com/author/daniel-robertson/*
54   James 1:19
55   https://www.goodreads.com/author/quotes/39628.Charles_F_Stanley
56   Cooper, Darien. *You Can Be the Wife of a Happy Husband*. p. 165-166.
57   Romans 8:31
58   http://www.betterthannewlyweds.com/tag/ruth-bell-graham/
59   Joshua 1:9
60   Retrieved from https://intentionaltoday.com/102-marriage-love-quotes-to-in
        spire-your-marriage/ Accessed May 2018.
61   Psalm 139:14
62   *Becoming One: Planning a Lasting, Joyful Marriage*, Don Meredith; Published July
        28th 1997 by Christian Family Life
63   Isaiah 43:25
64   John 11:39 NCV
65   Ephesians 5:33 *AMP*
66   Isaiah 59:2
67   Matthew 5:14
68   Matthew 7:5
69   nag 2018. In *Merriam-Webster.com*.
        Retrieved April, 2018, from https://www.merriam-webster.com/dictionary/sparkle
70   Luke 12:6
71   sparkle 2018. In *Merriam-Webster.com*.
        Retrieved April, 2018, from https://www.merriam-webster.com/dictionary/sparkle
72   Copyright © 2018 Anne Graham Lotz (AnGeL Ministries) Raleigh, North Carolina,
        USA. Used by permission. All rights reserved. www.annegrahamlotz.org
73   steadfast 2018. In *Merriam-Webster.com*.
        Retrieved July, 2018, from https://www.merriam-webster.com/dictionary/steadfast

Made in the USA
San Bernardino, CA
05 August 2019